THE
BIGGEST BIBLE
STORYBOOK

THE
BIGGEST BIBLE
STORYBOOK

100 favourite stories

written by Anne Adeney

illustrated by Ruth Rivers

Orion
Children's Books

Dedicated to my four wonderful daughters, Jenny, Libby, Katy and Megan,
with all my love, and the hope that you will all pass on
a love of Bible stories to your future children.

A. A.

For Anne, John and Maud

R. R.

First published in Great Britain in 2003
by Orion Children's Books
a division of the Orion Publishing Group Ltd
Orion House
5 Upper St Martin's Lane
London WC2H 9EA

Text copyright © Anne Adeney 2003
Illustrations copyright © Ruth Rivers 2003
Designed by Louise Millar

The right of Anne Adeney and Ruth Rivers to be identified
as the author and illustrator of this work has been asserted.

A catalogue record for this book is available from the British Library

Printed in Italy

ISBN 1 84255 029 2

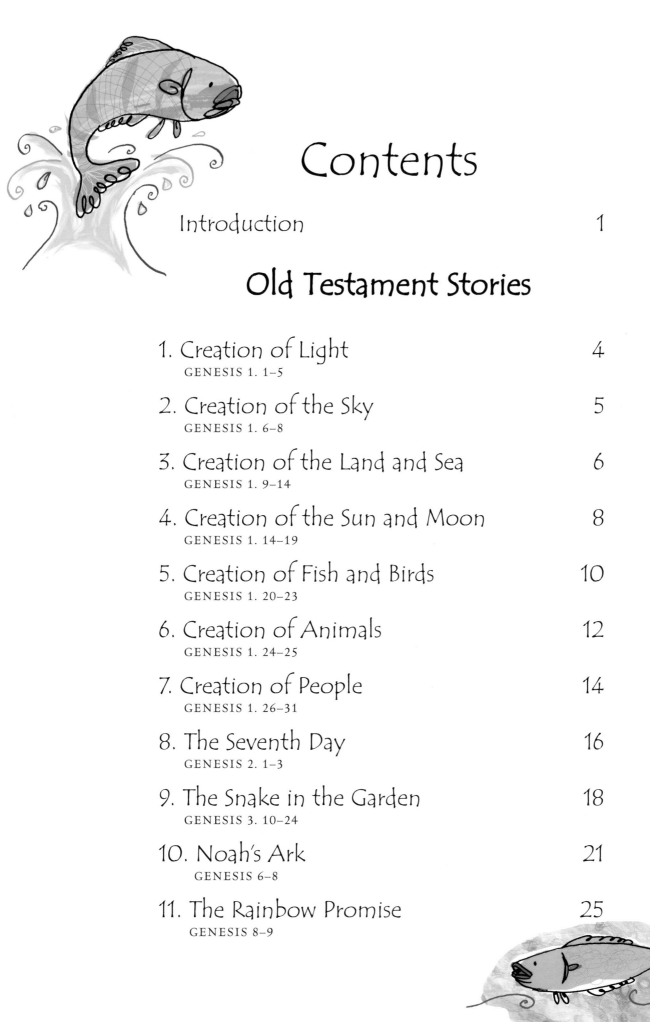

Contents

CONTENTS

New Testament Stories

CONTENTS

Introduction

I love to hear stories and to tell them too. The Bible is the biggest storybook in the whole world! It is really sixty-six different books all inside one cover, with thousands of stories, but I've picked out one hundred of the very best ones just for you.

I'm sure you like to hear stories too. Children have listened to stories since time began and then told them to someone else; maybe their friends, or their brothers and sisters. Then when they grow up, they tell the stories to their own children. This book is full of children telling the stories they have heard or even telling about things they have seen with their own eyes.

Although the stories take place over thousands of years, they all happened in the same region, to people of the same race. Children in the time of Jesus probably saw the same countryside as their ancestors in the days of Abraham. Many of the customs, festivals and pastimes were passed down through the ages and still survive in the Israel of the twenty-first century.

The storytellers are all children from long ago, so their way of life was very different from ours. There were no cars in Bible times, or TVs or books like this to read. Children your age even had jobs. They helped look after the animals, usually sheep, goats and donkeys. They helped their parents in their work as fishermen, carpenters, weavers or brickmakers. But even though their way of life was different, they were still children, just like you. They liked to hear stories and to tell them, to laugh, joke, and play.

In the early days of the Old Testament the people lived in tents and wandered round the countryside, always on the move, finding grass for their animals to eat. There are stories about life in those days. Later, people settled down and some of them became farmers. Then they lived in simple houses with one room, which they used for cooking, eating and sleeping. But they often had a flat roof, where the family would spend a lot of time. The children could play there and the women did their jobs, like grinding the grain to make flour for baking. In hot summers the roof was the coolest place to sleep.

The stories of the New Testament happened thousands of years after the Old Testament stories, around the time Jesus was alive. People lived in towns and cities then, as well as on farms. They would gather in the market-place to meet, shop and talk. The children would be there too, helping their parents or playing with their friends, but always watching and listening to what was going on, so that they could tell stories about everything they saw.

All the Bible stories really happened, a very long time ago. The stories were told over and over again and have been passed down through the ages to you. Maybe when you've heard one, you could tell it to someone else, to keep the stories moving through time. The children in this book loved hearing and telling these stories. I hope you do too.

Anne Adeney
Plymouth

EVA'S STORY

My name is Eva and I'm the grand-daughter of a goatherd. I live in the hills of Judah with my family.

'I wish I'd been there when the world was created!' I said. 'I wish I could have seen God make everything.'

'You're always wishing for something you can't have, Eva,' said my grand-mother, laughing. 'Why not just wish for a fig, like your brother? Anyway, there were no little girls around when God made the world. No grown-ups either, not even Adam and Eve.'

'Tell the story again, Grandmother!' I asked.

'I've no time for stories now, Eva!' said Grandmother, as she took up her strong stick. 'I must go and milk the goats and you must look after your little brother. You've heard the story often enough, why don't you be the storyteller and tell him?'

My brother was sitting outside our tent, eating the fig Grandmother had given him. I still remember that day when we sat together and I told Mo all the stories I knew about God creating the world. I told him a story for every year of my life. The first one was about the coming of light.

1
Creation of Light

Long, long ago, before the beginning of time, there was nothing except God. Then God made the heaven and the earth. He made heaven a bright, beautiful place. But the earth was dark and cold and empty. It didn't even have a shape.

So God decided that he wanted the earth to be a beautiful place as well. God can do *anything* at all, so he could create the world just as he wanted it. But the earth was as dark as could be, so on the very first day God said, 'Let there be light.'

Immediately light shone in the sky and some of the darkness went. But God is very wise. He knew that it would be just as bad to have all light as all darkness. So he kept some of the darkness. God said, 'I'll call the light *day* and the darkness *night*.' So that's how we got morning and evening. God looked at the day and the night that he had created and said, 'That is *good*!'

EVA'S STORY

'What happened next, Eva?' asked Mo.
'It's the story of what happened on the second day,' I said, 'when God made the sky. This is how he did it.'

2
Creation of the Sky

On the second day God looked at the earth. He could see it well now, because he'd created light. But all he could see was water. There was water everywhere. It covered the whole earth. So God said, 'There's too much water here, I need to separate it.'

Then God spoke and a huge blue space appeared above the waters covering the earth. 'I'll call this space *sky*,' said God.

There was still water above the earth, but God made big fluffy clouds to hold the water in the sky.

God looked at the sky and the clouds that he had created and said, 'That is *good!*'

EVA'S STORY

'What did God make next, Eva?' asked Mo.

'Well, it was the third day by then,' I said. 'There was day and night and sky and clouds, but there was no land for things to grow on. So next he had to create the land and the sea.'

3
Creation of the Land and Sea

God looked around the earth and he said, 'There's still too much water here. We need something different. I'm going to create some dry ground.'

So God spoke. That's all he had to do to make something happen. He just said, 'Let all the waters on the earth be gathered together,' and they were.

God looked at the waters and said, 'I'll call them *seas*.'

Then he could see all the dry ground sticking out between the seas. 'I'll call this dry ground *land*,' he said. God looked at the land and the seas and he was very pleased with what he had made.

God wanted plants to grow so he made soil to go on top of the land. He made rich black soil and fine brown soil. In some places he even made the soil red. He made squidgy clay and thick gooey mud. He made rocks of every size, from gigantic mountains to tiny grains of sand.

Then God said, 'Let the land grow every sort of grass and plant and flower and tree. Let everything have seeds inside it, so they will be able to grow again and again.'

Immediately forests of dark pine trees and orchards of trees bearing every sort of lovely fruit began to grow. Thick green grass carpeted the land and sweet-smelling meadows were filled with yellow buttercups and red poppies. He made steamy rain forests and dry sandy deserts, fields of delicious vegetables and bushes overloaded with soft fruit.

God looked at the sea and the land and all the plants and trees he had created and said, 'That is *good!*'

EVA'S STORY

'This is the story of what happened on the fourth day,' I told Mo.
    'Remember how I told you that God made light, so that he had
both light and darkness?'
    'Yes,' said Mo.
    'Well, next he made the sun, moon and stars.'

4
Creation of the Sun and Moon

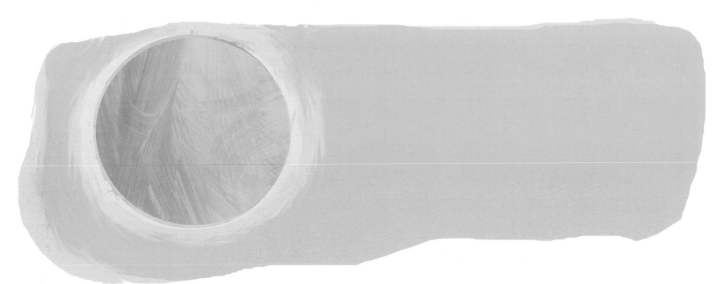

On the fourth day God decided he needed something to rule the
light and the darkness and divide them up. So he created the bright
golden sun to give light to the earth. He knew we would need sun-
light to keep us warm and to help plants to grow.

The sun controls the seasons too, so that spring always follows winter, summer follows spring, autumn follows summer and winter follows autumn.

God also created the silver moon to shine down on us and brighten the night. Then he flung stars into space so we could see them all glittering and shining in the dark sky. God looked at the sun and moon and stars that he had made and he was pleased. He saw how beautifully they shone and said, 'That is *good!*'

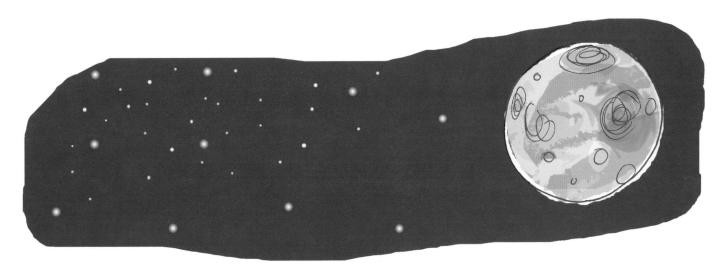

EVA'S STORY

'God made even more exciting things on the fifth day, so this is one of the stories I like best!' I said.

5
Creation of Fish and Birds

On the fifth day God looked at the sky and at the seas. Even though they were beautiful he knew there was something missing. I need some living things, he thought. So he said, 'Let there be fish in the sea!'

Suddenly the seas were full of fish and strange creatures. God made them every colour you can imagine, in thousands of strange shapes. Gigantic whales and tiny sea horses; long slithering eels and vast rays with fins like wings; spiny lobsters and scary squid. Every ocean, lake and river teemed with colourful creatures.

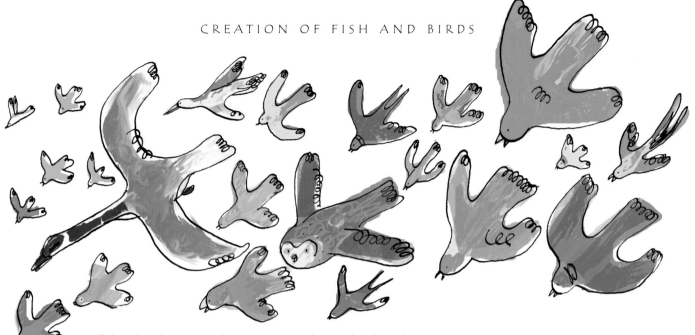

God looked up and said, 'Let there be birds in the sky!'

Immediately the skies were filled with birds of every kind and colour.

There were magnificent eagles flying over the mountains. Sea birds of all sorts swooped across the oceans. Tiny hummingbirds sipped nectar from the beautiful flowers. Huge ostriches galloped across the dry plains. Colourful parrots squawked in the steamy jungles.

God looked at the creatures he had made and he was very pleased. Then he did a very special thing. Just as he had done with the plants, he put inside each creature the seeds to make babies.

'Now my seas and my skies will always be filled with beautiful creatures,' he said. 'That is *good!*'

EVA'S STORY

'Now comes a story that's really exciting!' I told Mo. 'I'm going to tell you what happened on the sixth day. You know there's day and night, the sun, moon and stars, the sky full of birds and the seas full of fish. There's land covered with plants and trees, but nothing moved on the land. So this is what God did next.'

6
Creation of Animals

'Let there be all sorts of animals on the land!' said God, looking at his new world.

Instantly there were animals everywhere. Sheep, goats and donkeys grazed in the fields. Up in the mountains, bears climbed and leopards prowled. In the jungles were chattering monkeys and magnificent lions. Across the plains roamed tall giraffes, massive elephants with long trunks and graceful antelopes. Even the sandy deserts were full of camels, lizards and snakes. There were cats and dogs, mice and rabbits, locusts and buzzing bumblebees.

God made so many different animals it would take days to name them all. He put seeds inside each one so that forever afterwards there would be puppies and kittens, piglets and cubs and baby animals of all kinds. He looked at the animals he had made and he was very pleased.

'That is *good!*' he said.

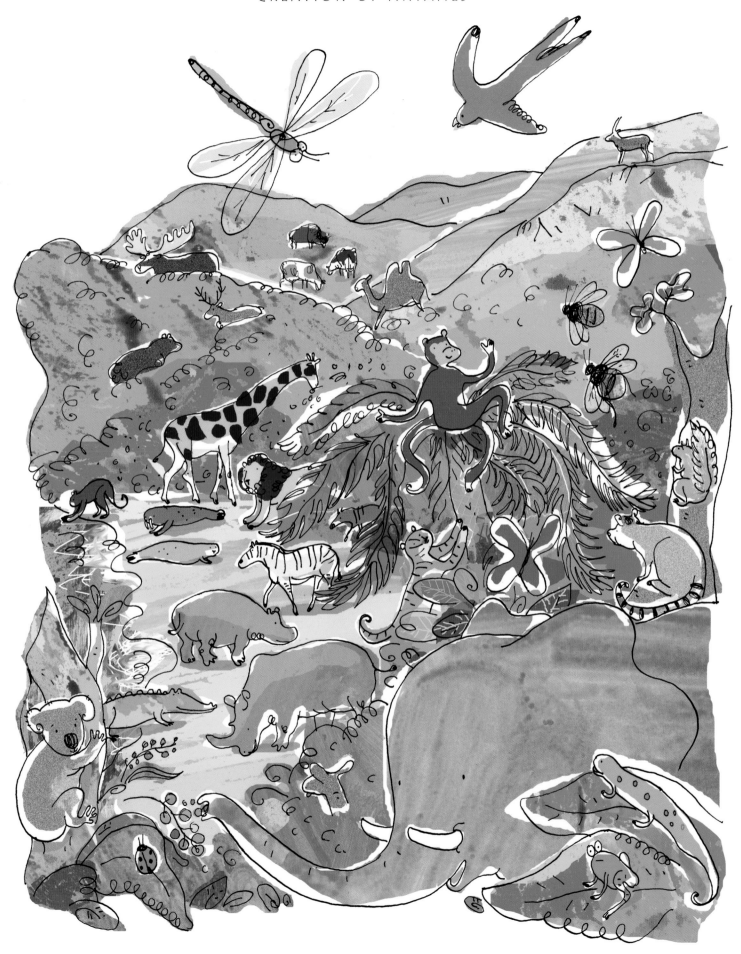

EVA'S STORY

'What happened then, Eva?' asked Mo.

'I haven't even finished the sixth day yet! The most important thing is still to come,' I said. 'God looked at everything he had made and he knew all of it was good, but there was still something missing. So he made Adam and Eve!'

'Adam and Eve had babies too, didn't they, Eva?' said Mo excitedly.

'Of course they did! Great-grandmother Eve had children and they had children and their children had children for years until Grandmother had Abba, our daddy. And he had me and named me after Eve and the last baby of all . . . was you.'

Mo thought of all those babies from Adam and Eve to himself and smiled a great big smile.

7
Creation of People

'I need someone to look after this world I have made,' said God. 'I will make people to look something like myself.'

So he took some clay and shaped it into a body and breathed life into it. It became a man who could live and breathe, walk and talk. 'I will call you Adam,' said God happily. 'I have made thousands of plants and animals, insects, birds and sea creatures for you. Now I want *you* to give them all names.'

So Adam named everything he saw. Although he could talk to the friendly animals, they couldn't talk back. There was nothing there like him. God knew that Adam would be lonely without somebody else, so he made a woman to be his friend and helper.

'Your name will be *Eve*,' he said. 'Together you will have babies and when they grow up they will have children of their own. One day the whole earth will be full of people you have made. They may look different, because they'll be black and white, brown and yellow, but they'll all be something like me. I'm putting you two in charge of the earth and all the plants and animals I have made. You must take good care of them for me.'

God looked at the people he had made and he was very pleased. 'That is *very good!*' he said.

EVA'S STORY

'Now there's a short story for the seventh day, because God had finished making everything by then,' I said.

'Did God really make everything in just six days?' asked Mo.

'I asked Father about that. He said that God made everything before time began, so we don't know how long his days lasted. They weren't the same as our day, from getting up one morning, doing things all day, going to sleep and waking up again. His day might be as short as the time it takes you to eat a fig, or as long as millions of years! Anyway, this is what happened.'

8
The Seventh Day

The creation of the heaven and the earth was now finished. There was light and darkness; land and sea; sun, moon and stars; fish, birds and animals and even people to look after it all.

So on the seventh day God rested from his work and enjoyed looking at everything he had done. He knew that everyone would need a break from hard work and so he decided to put a rest day into his plan for his world. He blessed the seventh day and said, 'This day shall be called the *Sabbath*. It will be a holy day when my people can rest.'

EVA'S STORY

'How do you *know* all those things, Eva?' asked Mo.

'Grandmother has told me the stories hundreds of times,' I said. 'She heard them from her grandmother, who heard them from hers – right back to Great-Grandmother Eve.'

'Where did Eve hear them, then?' asked Mo.

'I don't know,' I replied. 'Perhaps God himself told her. Maybe when they were walking together in the Garden of Eden.'

'What's the Garden of Eden?' asked Mo.

'That's my last story,' I said.

9
The Snake in the Garden

Adam and Eve lived happily in the garden that God had made for them. It was a paradise, with lots of really friendly animals. They saw a lion cub playing with a little lamb and bears dancing with butterflies. The Garden of Eden was full of gorgeous flowers and wonderful trees, which produced the most delicious fruit imaginable.

It was warm and pleasant in the garden, so Adam and Eve didn't need to wear any clothes. They were quite happy to walk around naked and enjoy the golden sunshine and swim in the clear rivers that flowed through Eden to water the splendid plants. They could just reach out and pick lovely fruit from the trees without any effort at all. But there was a special tree in the middle of the garden that God had warned Adam about.

'This is the Tree of Knowledge', said God. 'It has the only fruit which you are forbidden to eat. If you eat it, you will die.'

Adam and Eve had so much good food from the other trees that they never thought of disobeying God and eating the forbidden fruit. Then one day a snake slithered over to talk to Eve. He was the craftiest creature God had made and he tried his hardest to get Eve into trouble.

'I'm sure you won't really die if you eat this fruit', said the snake. 'I think it will make you as clever as God himself. You will be just like him and know what is good and what is evil.'

Eve was really tempted. So she got up and picked the fruit. She ate some right away and it was so delicious that she offered it to Adam.

'Here, Adam, have a bite!' she said. 'This fruit will make us as wise as God. Surely that will be a good thing.'

Adam took the fruit and finished it off. It was good. But when he'd finished it, Adam and Eve looked at each and realised something for the first time.

'We've got no clothes on!' said Eve. 'Quick, hide behind that bush while I make us something out of those big fig leaves!'

When God came to walk in the garden that evening he found Adam and Eve still hiding behind the trees, scared to come out and see him.

'Why are you hiding?' asked God.

'We don't want you to see us because we are naked,' said Adam shamefully.

'Who told you that you were naked?' asked God sternly. 'Have you eaten the forbidden fruit?'

'I did eat some,' admitted Adam. 'But it was Eve's fault. She gave it to me!'

'It wasn't my fault!' said Eve. 'The snake tricked me into eating it!'

God was very angry that Adam and Eve had disobeyed him and were already bringing unhappiness and fighting into his perfect garden.

'You must leave my garden and never return,' said God. 'If you had obeyed me you could have lived in this beautiful place for ever. Instead you will have to work hard to grow crops from weedy ground, full of stones and thistles, until eventually you will die.'

So God gave them animal skins to wear and sent them out of the garden for ever. He set angels with flaming swords to guard the gates of Eden. Adam and Eve knew that, because of their disobedience, they would never have such an easy, happy life again.

SHEM'S STORY

My name is Shem and my great-grandfather is a famous storyteller. He is so old now that his voice shakes when he talks, but he still tells the most amazing stories about what happened to him when he was young. His name is Shem, like mine, so perhaps I'll be a storyteller too. Or maybe a boat builder, like his father, Noah. But Noah only built a boat because God told him to.

10
Noah's Ark

People had become so wicked that God was sorry he ever made them. But Noah still loved God and obeyed him. One day God called to Noah.

'I'm going to send an enormous flood to wash away all these wicked people. So I want you to build a huge boat and save the animals.'

'But what about my family, Lord?' asked Noah. 'Please don't destroy them! And how will I build a boat big enough for *all* the animals? It's impossible!'

'Don't worry, Noah,' said God. 'You can take the whole family with you. You'll need them to help look after the animals. I'll tell you exactly how big to build the boat and guide you every step of the way. Of course you couldn't fit all the animals in! But you must take a male and a female of each kind, then they can have babies later on. Now you must start collecting wood for the boat and food for yourselves and the animals.'

So Noah got to work. He called to his sons.

'Ham, fetch me my tools, we're going to build a boat! Shem and Japheth, start cutting down trees and hauling the wood back here. Get your wives to start collecting food; we'll be making a long journey. And tar! Fetch tar to make the boat waterproof!'

So, with the help of his sons, Noah began work on the huge boat, called an ark. It took a long time to build, because it was so big. But at last it was finished. God sent a male and female of every sort of animal and Noah led them, two by two, on to the ark. Then God called Noah again.

'Get on board, Noah. In a week's time I'm going to make it rain for forty days and forty nights. But you'll be safe in the ark.'

So Noah and his wife and his sons and their wives said goodbye to the land they had lived on all their lives and climbed on board the enormous ark. Noah had all the pairs of animals aboard, plus seven pairs of all the birds. He would need these to make sacrifices to God.

The skies went black and rain poured down. The rivers and springs gushed out water from the depths of the earth until even the mountains were covered. Every bad person was drowned. But the ark floated unharmed on the raging waters.

After one hundred and fifty days God sent a wind across the waters and the floods began to disappear. The ark came to rest on the mountains of Ararat. But it was months before the waters went down enough for the trees to grow again. Noah kept sending out his birds to look for dry ground. He sent out a dove, which flew around for miles. But it could not find a dry place to land, so it returned to the ark.

Seven days later Noah sent the dove out again. When it came back to him that evening it had a fresh olive branch in its beak. A week later he sent it out again and this time it did not come back. Noah knew that it had found a dry place to roost and soon it would be safe for the animals to leave the ark.

SHEM'S STORY

I love to listen to my great-grandfather's stories about his life. I've often wondered what it was like for him, living with Noah and all those animals on the ark for such a long time. It's an incredible story!

11
The Rainbow Promise

Noah and his family had lived on the ark for months and months. Already, many of the animals had produced babies and it was getting very crowded. Everyone kept asking Noah when they could leave the ark.

'Just look out there,' said Noah. 'We can see lots of land now. Last week the dove came back with an olive branch in her beak. I sent her out again this morning and she hasn't come back. That must mean she's found a good place to roost. Soon it will be our turn. At least the land here will grow crops well when it dries out. We must have shovelled tons of manure overboard by now!'

But it was another twelve weeks before the ground was dry enough to live on. Then God came and spoke to Noah.

'You can leave the ark now, Noah. Release all the animals and reptiles and birds so they can go and make new homes on the dry land and raise their young.'

So Noah set all the animals free and soon the ark was empty, apart from the smell, which lingered for many months. Noah and his family climbed down the gangplank and looked at the new land God had brought them to. As Noah had guessed, it was very fertile.

'The first thing we must do is build an altar to give thanks to God for saving us from the flood,' said Noah.

So that's what they did. God was pleased with the offering they made on the altar and made this promise.

'Even though I know that there will be bad people again in the future, I will never send a flood like this to wipe out the whole world. As long as the earth remains, springtime will come and you can harvest your crops. The cold winter will follow the hot summer every year, just as day follows night. You and your family must make a new start, Noah. The world and its animals are yours, but you must look after them and use them wisely.'

'So we'll never have such terrible rain again?' asked Noah.

'Of course it will rain again!' said God. 'You need rain to make the crops grow. But if it ever rains so much that you begin to worry that I've forgotten my promise, just look up into the sky. I will put a rainbow there as a sign for you. Every time you see the beautiful colours of the rainbow shining amongst the black rain clouds, you will remember my promise.'

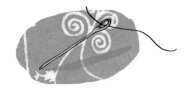

JAVAN'S STORY

My name is Javan and my whole family works for Abraham, a rich man with so many sheep and goats that you could never count them in one day. My father makes all the tents that Abraham and his household live in and the rest of us help him mend them when they get ripped or worn.

You get to hear everything that's going on when you're mending tents. That's how I found out that we were going on a long journey. God actually spoke to Abraham and told him to move all his family and animals to a new land.

12
Abraham's Journey

God said to Abraham, 'You must journey to Canaan. There I will make you the father of a great nation.'

Abraham was already an old man of seventy-five. He had no children, but he believed what God said. So he got his servants to round up the flocks and load everything he owned on to camels. Then he took his wife Sarah and his nephew Lot, and left. It was a long hard journey, with many stops. There was a famine and nobody had enough to eat. So Abraham took all his people to Egypt, but the Pharaoh, the ruler of Egypt, was angry with Abraham and sent them out of Egypt under armed escort.

They travelled again, until they came to the land of Canaan, where they settled down. But Lot was a rich man too and had big flocks like Abraham's. There were so many animals that there was not enough grass for them to eat. Fights began to break out between Lot's herdsmen and Abraham's as to whose animals should be allowed to graze.

Abraham knew that families shouldn't fight, so he said to Lot, 'We should split up now. You can choose which land you want first.'

So Lot looked around and thought that the fertile Jordan valley looked like the Garden of Eden. He decided to settle there, while Abraham and his servants stayed in Canaan.

JARED'S STORY

My name is Jared and my father is a brickmaker in the town of Shiloh.

'Watch me make bricks!' I said to Enoch. He's my little brother. I took the square brick mould full of squishy mud. Then I tapped it hard and the square of mud slipped out neatly. Soon I had long rows of mud bricks ready to bake dry in the hot sun. Father would be pleased with me. He has to make thousands and thousands of bricks to build new houses.

I love making bricks to build houses to make towns and cities. Yet I also know the story of how whole cities were destroyed, but a good man was saved.

13
The Wicked City

The people who lived in the cities of Sodom and Gomorrah didn't respect God and did wicked things all the time. So God decided to destroy the cities and their people. Abraham was horrified when God told him. His nephew Lot and his family lived there and he didn't want them to die.

'You're a fair and merciful God,' said Abraham. 'If you find fifty good people there, will you promise not to destroy it?'

'The people are very evil,' said God. 'But if I find fifty good people I won't destroy it.'

Then Abraham tried to bargain, in case there were not enough good people. In the end God said, 'If there are only ten good people there I will not destroy the city.'

That evening Lot saw two strangers at the city gate. He knew that the people of the city were so bad that they would do the men great harm, so he asked them home for supper.

'Don't worry about us,' said the men. 'We'll just camp out here.'

'Please come to my house and stay the night,' Lot said. 'It'll be no trouble.'

At last they agreed and went home with Lot. But after supper a big gang gathered outside Lot's house. They'd heard that he was entertaining strangers and wanted him to put them out on the street so they could ill-treat them.

Lot went out and begged them not to be so wicked. But the gang were determined to break in and get the two men. They would even have killed Lot. He and his family were in great danger.

The two men reached out, pulled Lot inside, and locked and bolted the door. The gang yelled and raged outside and were still determined to get them. But although the men looked just like ordinary men, they were really messengers sent from God. They made the gang blind for a while, so they couldn't even find the door of Lot's house and break in.

31

JAVED'S STORY

'You can put the mud into the moulds, Enoch,' I said. 'Then I'll tap it out on to the ground. If we help Father make lots of bricks he'll be able to buy a kiln. We'll build a fire inside the kiln and the bricks will dry out much quicker. Then we'll be the best brickmakers in the whole city!'

'But, Jared, what happened in the story?' asked Enoch. 'Did the wicked men get Lot?'

14
Lot's Wife

God's messengers grabbed Lot and pulled him back into his house, to save him from the angry mob. Lot was very confused 'What's happening?' he asked.

'God hasn't found even ten good men in this evil city,' said the messenger, 'so he has sent us to destroy it and every wicked person who lives here. You must hurry away with your family before it's too late!'

Lot was amazed and frightened. When dawn broke next morning, he still didn't know what to do. Would God really destroy his home and even his whole city? He knew how wicked everyone was, but it was still hard to believe.

Seeing his hesitation, the two messengers grabbed Lot and his wife and two daughters by the hands and led them from the city.

'Be quick!' they urged the family. 'Time is running out! Run towards the hills where you'll be safe! The most important thing to remember is this – don't look back!'

As the sun rose, Lot and his family fled for their lives. God rained down fire from heaven on to the cities of Sodom and Gomorrah. All the buildings and all the people were destroyed. But God saved Lot because he was a good man and had always obeyed him.

But Lot's wife did not obey God's messengers. She couldn't resist taking a last look back towards the city. And the minute she looked back she was turned into a statue made of solid salt.

ASHER'S STORY

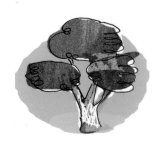

I am Asher, a butcher's son. One day Abraham asked me to help him catch the fattest calf, and to get my father to prepare it, while Sarah his wife made some pancakes. Three guests had arrived and he wanted to give them the tenderest meat. My father always does the butchering for Abraham's tribe so I am used to helping him prepare the meat. Little did I know that one of those guests was the most important I could ever serve.

15
A Son at Last

Abraham hurried to bring food to the three unexpected guests, who had seemed to appear out of nowhere. He served them roast veal and fresh pancakes as they rested under some shady trees.

'Where's Sarah your wife?' asked one of the men.

'She's in the tent,' replied Abraham, knowing that Sarah was actually listening behind the tent flap.

Now this man was really God. He told Abraham, 'When I come back here in nine months' time, Sarah will have a baby boy!'

In the tent, Sarah laughed. What a silly thing to say! She was much too old to have a baby, and Abraham was really ancient, all of a hundred years old!

Then God said to Abraham, 'Why did your wife laugh just then?

Nothing is too difficult for God. I promise you will have a son and he will be the father of nations.'

'I didn't laugh!' said Sarah, because she was embarrassed and afraid that this was really God.

But God did not hold it against her and nine months later she gave birth to a baby boy. Abraham was delighted that God had kept his promise. He named the boy Isaac, which means 'he laughs', because his wife Sarah had laughed at God's promise of a son in their old age.

OMAR'S STORY

My name is Omar and I live with my family in the Jordan valley. One day my little brother Kenan and I were watching the priest at work.

'People have brought lots of animals to the priest today,' said Kenan, watching the smoke billowing up from the fire. 'But he's not cooking them properly. They're burning up!'

'He's not cooking them, he's offering them to God,' I said. 'People bring animals or grain to the priest to burn when they want to thank God for something, or to say they are sorry for something bad that they've done.'

Then I remembered the story about how Abraham was asked to sacrifice his most treasured possession.

16
Sacrificing Isaac

Abraham really loved his son Isaac, who had grown to be a strong boy. But God decided to test Abraham's faith.

'Take Isaac up into the mountains and kill him as a sacrifice to me,' said God.

How do you think Abraham felt when he heard that? But he trusted God, so next day he got up early and chopped wood for the fire. He got two servants to stack the wood on a donkey, woke Isaac and the four of them set out on a three-day journey to the mountains.

'You two stay here,' Abraham said. 'Isaac and I will go and worship God and come back later.' So Isaac carried the wood, while Abraham carried the knife and something to start a fire.

'Where's the lamb for the sacrifice?' asked Isaac.

'God will see to that,' said Abraham.

When they reached the right place Abraham used a big flat stone for an altar. He put the wood on the altar, ready for the fire. Then he tied Isaac up and gently laid him on the wood for a sacrifice. He lifted the knife high, summoning the courage to kill his son.

Suddenly a voice called out to him from heaven, 'Abraham! Abraham! Don't hurt Isaac! You have proved that God comes first with you by being willing to sacrifice what you love most.'

Abraham heaved a great sigh of relief. He noticed a ram caught by its horns in the bushes. So he took it and sacrificed it to God in Isaac's place. Then he and Isaac and the servants went safely back home.

Abraham called the place 'God provides' and it is still called that to this day.

REBECCA'S STORY

My name is Rebecca and my father grows cucumbers and melons. I have a twin sister called Rachel and we've always been good friends, unlike some fighting twins I've heard about! While I was helping Grandmother grind the wheat for tomorrow's bread I asked her who I was named after. She told me the story of how Isaac found his wife, Rebecca, and how they had their twin boys.

17
Fighting Twins

Abraham was very old now, so he thought he'd find his son Isaac a wife. He thought the best women came from Mesopotamia, where his brother lived, so he sent his oldest servant to find a bride.

'God will help you find the right woman and bring her back here,' he told the servant.

The servant went to the city and stopped to rest his camels by a well, where the women come to get water. He prayed to God to give him a sign to show which was the right woman for Isaac.

'When I ask for a drink of water, let the right woman offer to water my camels too,' he said to God.

A beautiful young woman called Rebecca came down to the well and the servant asked her for a drink.

'Certainly, sir, you look hot and tired! And I'll give your camels a drink as well,' said Rebecca kindly.

The servant knew then that Rebecca was the right wife for Isaac. He gave her the fine ring and two gold bracelets that Abraham had sent for her and asked if he could stay with her father that night.

When they got to her house, the servant found that her father was Abraham's nephew. He told her family the story of how God had helped him find a wife for Isaac and they were happy to agree to the marriage. When the servant took Rebecca home, Isaac was delighted. He fell in love with her at once and married her immediately.

Isaac and his wife Rebecca didn't have any children for many years, then she became pregnant with twins. Even before they were born Rebecca felt as if a wrestling match was going on inside her body! God told Isaac that he planned to make the younger twin the head of the family.

The first boy was so hairy, he looked as if he was born wearing a red fur coat! They called him Esau, which means 'Hairy'. The second boy was born hanging on to his brother's foot, so they called him Jacob, which means 'Grabber'.

When the boys grew up Esau was his father's favourite because he was a good hunter, but Rebecca adored Jacob, who stayed behind quietly in the tents with his mother.

ZILPAH'S STORY

My name is Zilpah and my family are shepherds in the hills near Kedesh. One day my sister had just left to take lunch up to our brother Malachi, who was minding our sheep on the hillside. I saw she'd left something behind.

'You've forgotten the water!' I shouted, but Judith was already out of sight. It was a hot day, so I ran after her with the goatskin water bag. Judith soon came into sight and I watched as she stopped and unwrapped the fig leaves from the barley cakes I had given her.

She smelt one and I knew she was longing to eat it. Then there would only be two left for Malachi, who was always hungry! Judith sighed, wrapped up the barley cakes again and went on her way. I was so pleased that she had not cheated Malachi out of part of his dinner. He might never have found out, but it would still have been cheating. Just like the story I heard about a real cheat.

18
Jacob the Cheat

When Isaac was very old, he knew it was close to his time to die. He wanted to put his affairs in order, so he said, 'Esau, take your bow and arrows and go hunting so you can prepare a last good meal for me and I can bless you before I die.'

Rebecca heard this and said to Jacob, 'Let's trick your father into believing that you are Esau and then he'll give you his blessing to be head of the family.'

'He may be nearly blind, but he can still feel,' said Jacob. 'My skin is smooth and Esau is so hairy that he'll never believe I'm my brother!'

But Rebecca had a plan. She made Jacob put on Esau's best clothes and wrapped goatskins around his neck and arms. Then he took a delicious meal Rebecca had cooked to his father and asked for his blessing.

'Who are you?' asked his blind father.

'I'm Esau!' Jacob replied. 'I've brought that good food you asked for.'

'Come and let me feel you to make sure,' said Isaac. 'I don't think you've had time to hunt a deer *and* cook it!'

But when Jacob came close Isaac felt the hairy goatskin, smelt Esau's smell from the clothes and thought it was Esau. He gave Jacob his blessing and put him in charge of the family when he died.

When Esau came home from hunting, Isaac was shocked to find that he'd been tricked. But it was too late. Isaac could not take back the blessings he had given Jacob, even if he wanted to.

'I'm going to kill Jacob!' yelled Esau.

But Rebecca sent Jacob off to visit his uncle, where he would be safe from Esau's anger.

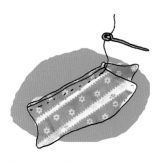

DEBORAH'S STORY

My name is Deborah and I live in a village beside the Sea of Galilee. Today I was with my sisters and cousins, having a sewing lesson with my grandmother.

'I hate sewing!' wailed my smallest sister, as she pricked her finger for the third time. 'I'll never be any good at it!'

'All girls must learn to sew,' said Grandmother, 'otherwise we'd all have to wear animal skins like they did in olden times!'

We all giggled at the thought of that, glad of our woollen tunics, sleeveless coats and linen head cloths. But at least we could sit round in a circle together, laughing and chatting as we learnt to sew. Grandmother always told us stories and my favourite was the one about a very unusual coat, which belonged to a boy called Joseph.

19

Joseph and his Coat of Many Colours

Jacob had twelve sons, but the youngest, whose name was Joseph, was the one he loved best. Jacob gave Joseph a very special coat. It was unusual, not only because it was woven in many different colours, but because it had long sleeves. His older brothers were jealous because they hadn't been given special presents, so they hated Joseph.

Joseph worked as a shepherd with his brothers, and whenever they did anything wrong, he went home and told his father about it. This tale-telling made them hate Joseph even more.

Then Joseph started having dreams and was eager to tell his brothers about them.

'Last night I dreamt that we were all tying up sheaves of wheat when my sheaf stood up straight in the field and all your sheaves bowed down to mine.'

'Do you really think you're going to rule over us like that?' they asked, hating Joseph still more.

'I've had another dream!' he said, a few days later. 'I dreamt that the sun, moon and eleven stars bowed down to me!'

His brothers got very angry and even his father was cross about his boasting.

'Do you really think that your mother and I and all your brothers are going to bow down to you?' he said. But once he'd calmed down he thought about Joseph's strange dreams. He wondered if God had somehow chosen Joseph to be a leader, even though he was the youngest son. Perhaps the dreams would come true after all.

BUZ'S STORY

My name is Buz and I'm a camel boy. I work with my brother beside a well on the route of the traders.

'I'll ride at the head of a camel caravan one day,' I told my brother as he hauled on the rope to draw the bucket from the well. 'The long line of camels following me will be carrying exciting things from the East – colourful cloth, gum, balm and expensive myrrh. They'll all belong to me and I'll protect them from robbers with my shiny sword!'

'Take these buckets of water to the camels, Buz, or you'll never grow up to be the leader,' said my brother.

I took the water over to the camels, which had travelled so far without a drop to drink.

'Maybe I'll even find somebody exciting, like when Grandfather bought Joseph, who became such a famous man,' I said dreamily.

20
Joseph is Sold into Slavery

Joseph was his father's favourite son and this made all his brothers very jealous. One day the older brothers were out looking after the sheep, when Jacob called Joseph to him.

'Your brothers are all in the fields with the sheep, Joseph,' said Jacob. 'Go and see what they're up to for me.'

So Joseph set out, but his brothers saw him coming.

'Let's kill that awful Joseph, and throw his body down a well!' said Levi.

'We'll tell Father he was eaten by a lion!' said Judah.

'Don't kill him, put him down an empty well to starve,' said Reuben, the eldest, who was just leaving. He secretly planned to come back and rescue Joseph.

As soon as Joseph arrived, his brothers took his fine coat of many colours, then threw him down a well. They sat down to eat, ignoring his cries for help. Soon, a long line of camels came by. It was traders on their way to Egypt.

'Let's sell Joseph to those traders,' said Judah. 'Then we'll get some money as well as getting rid of that annoying dreamer!'

So they pulled Joseph out of the well and sold him for twenty silver coins. When Reuben came back and found the well empty, he was very upset. The brothers had covered up what they had done by tearing Joseph's coat and dipping it in goat's blood. They took it back home and showed their father.

'Oh no!' cried Jacob. 'That's Joseph's coat! He must have been attacked and eaten by a wild animal!'

Nobody could comfort Jacob, for he had lost his favourite son. He did not know that Joseph was now a slave in the household of the King of Egypt.

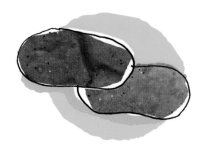

IRA'S STORY

I'm Ira and I work in a baker's shop in Hebron. I'm glad my job isn't grinding flour. It's hard work and I'd be scared of getting my fingers caught between the stones. It's so dusty too! Someone sieves the flour, then passes it on to the next boy, who mixes it with water and yeast to make dough. The baker always likes to do the next bit himself, because he says it's the most important. He kneads the dough, then shapes it into round loaves.

My job comes next. I take the bread stamp by its handle and press it into each loaf in turn. It's the easiest job in the bakery, even though the wooden stamp is quite heavy. While I'm stamping the loaves, ready for the oven, the baker likes me to repeat the tales my mother tells me at home. His favourite one has a bit about the king of Egypt's baker, who came to a nasty end.

21
Joseph and the Pharaoh

Joseph's brothers were so jealous of him that they sold him to some slave traders on their way to Egypt. When the traders reached Egypt, they sold Joseph into the household of the Pharaoh, who was Egypt's king. At first he did very well but then his master's wife had him put into prison. Here he met Pharaoh's wine steward and chief baker. They'd both made Pharaoh angry, so he'd locked them up.

One night, both men had very strange dreams. Joseph told the wine steward, 'Your dream about squeezing the juice from grapes on three branches into the Pharaoh's cup means that in three days you'll get your job back.'

'What about my dream?' the baker asked eagerly. 'I dreamt that I was carrying three boxes of cakes on my head, but birds were eating the pastries in the top box.'

'I'm afraid it's bad news', said Joseph sadly. 'Your dream means that in three days Pharaoh will have you killed and throw your body to the birds to eat.'

It happened exactly as Joseph had said. Two years later, the Pharaoh himself had a strange dream. The wine steward told him about Joseph, so Pharaoh asked him to explain the dream.

'Only God knows the meaning of dreams', said Joseph. 'Tell me about it and God will help me explain.'

Pharaoh told him about seven thin cows who ate seven fat cows and seven ripe ears of corn, which were swallowed up by seven thin scrawny ones. God gave Joseph the explanation.

'God is telling you that after seven good years there will be seven bad years of famine, when no crops will grow', said Joseph. 'You must save food wisely so your people will have enough to eat.'

Pharaoh thought Joseph was so clever that he put him in charge. For seven years, the crops grew well. Joseph travelled around the country, collecting the extra grain and storing it safely. When the famine came there was enough food to give to the starving people of Egypt.

There was no food in Canaan either, so Jacob sent his sons to Egypt to find some. Joseph forgave his brothers and used his power to help his family, even though they had sold him into slavery.

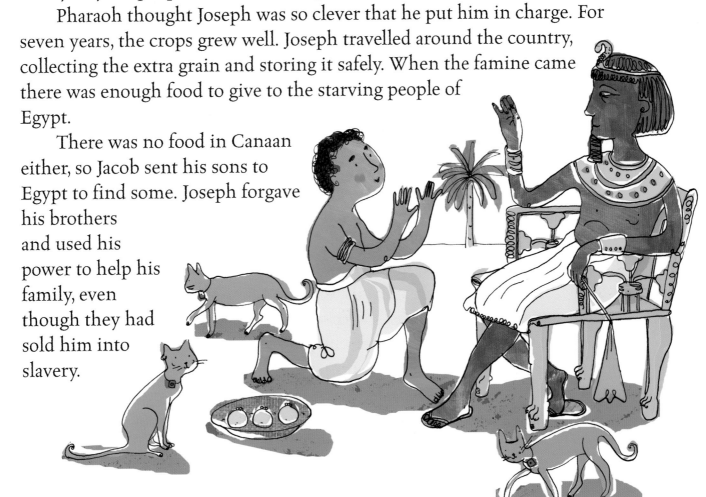

MIRIAM'S STORY

My name is Miriam and all my family weave baskets. My ancestors used to live in Egypt, which was a very scary thing at the time, because they were all slaves. The one I like to hear and tell about most is Miriam. It's partly because we share the same name and are both good at weaving baskets. But it's mostly because her quick thinking saved the family from losing her baby brother when he was tiny.

22
The Baby in the Bulrushes

Pharaoh was frightened of the Israelites. Even though he had made them slaves, he was worried because there were so many of them. 'Send for all the women who help the Israelite women have their babies!' he roared.

When all the midwives came he gave them an order.

'Every time a Hebrew woman has a boy baby you are to kill it!'

But the midwives feared God more than the Pharaoh and let the new baby boys live, even though Pharaoh wanted them thrown into the river to feed the huge crocodiles that lived there.

One Hebrew woman had a lovely baby boy. She managed to keep him hidden until he was three months old, but then he grew so strong and cried so vigorously that she could hide him no longer.

'Go and gather some papyrus reeds from the river, Miriam,' said the mother to her daughter. 'Then you can help me weave a strong basket.'

They made the basket, then the mother gently laid her baby boy inside and pushed it out into the river Nile.

'Watch out for him, Miriam!' she said, with tears in her eyes. 'Make sure no crocodiles get him!'

Miriam ran along the bank, keeping close watch on the basket. When she heard voices she hid in the reeds. Pharaoh's daughter had come down to the river and heard the baby's sudden cry.

'It's a poor little Hebrew baby!' she said, as her servants took the baby out and unwrapped him for her to see. 'I'd like to look after him, but he's so tiny!'

Miriam bravely went up to the princess and said, 'Shall I go and fetch a Hebrew woman who can feed the baby and look after him for you while he is so little?'

The princess agreed and Miriam ran to fetch her mother.

'Look after this baby and I will pay you well!' said the princess. 'I'll call him Moses, because that means "drawn out of the water".'

So Moses had his own mother to care for him and a clever older sister to play with him.

MIRIAM'S STORY

Reeds and grasses can be woven into all sorts of things. I have only learned to make mats and baskets so far. But my parents make really difficult things. Sandals are hard to weave, but of course everyone needs them to protect their feet from the stony ground, so they make lots of them.

Moses had to take his sandals off when he met God in the burning bush, because it was holy ground. I wonder if he had sandals like the ones my mother weaves?

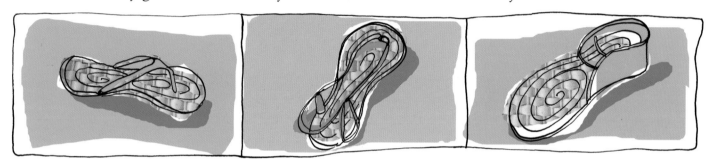

23
The Burning Bush

Moses left Egypt when he was grown-up and became a shepherd. One day he was looking after his sheep when he saw a bush on fire. He went closer to warm himself and was amazed to see that although there were lots of flames the bush wasn't burning away.

Suddenly the voice of God called out from inside the bush, 'Don't come any closer, Moses! This is holy ground. Take your sandals off! I am the God of Abraham, Isaac and Jacob!'

Moses hid his face, for he was afraid to look at God.

'I have heard the cries of my people suffering in slavery in Egypt,' said God, 'and I've chosen you to go to Pharaoh and tell him to let them go!'

'Why choose me?' asked Moses in alarm. 'Nobody will believe that God has sent me. If I say I've seen you, they'll just call me a liar!'

'Throw your rod upon the ground!' said God.

Moses threw down the big stick and instantly God turned it into a writhing snake. Moses ran away as quickly as he could.

'Come back and pick it up by the tail,' said God.

Nervously Moses picked up the snake, which turned back into a rod again. God gave Moses other signs to prove to the people that he had seen God, but still Moses made excuses.

'I won't know what to say!' he pleaded. 'Please send someone else!'

'Don't you trust me to tell you what to say?' said God angrily. 'Your brother Aaron is a good speaker. You will go to Egypt together and he can do the talking.'

So Moses set out on his difficult task.

JAKE'S STORY

I'm Jake and my father owns a vineyard. The job in my father's vineyard that I love watching best is treading the grapes. I help pour the baskets of grapes into the big stone winepress, then the men jump into the winepress and squash the grapes with their bare feet. I'd love to do it too, but I'm not tall enough yet.

'It will be a few years yet before you can reach up to hold on to the ropes hanging from the wooden beam, Jake,' says my father.

Suddenly hard cold hail pelts down from the grey sky. We run for shelter and watch it rain down on the vineyard.

'This won't do my vines any good at all,' says Father gloomily. 'I'd say it was the worst hail I've ever seen!'

As I watch the hailstones rain down I think about the hailstones and other plagues sent to Egypt.

24
The Plagues of Egypt

Moses and Aaron had been given a task by God. They journeyed to Egypt to see the Pharaoh and give him God's message. 'God doesn't want the Israelites to be slaves,' they told him. 'You must let my people go!'

But Pharaoh wouldn't let them go. He was so angry that he made them work even harder. So God told Moses to go back to Pharaoh and ask him again. Aaron threw down his rod before the king and it became a hissing snake.

'My magicians can do just as well!' said the king and he wouldn't listen to Moses.

God made the River Nile turn from water into blood. The fish all died and nobody could drink. But Pharaoh still wouldn't let the Israelites go.

Then God sent a plague of frogs. Everywhere you looked there were thousands of frogs! There were frogs in people's beds, in their ovens and in their food.

'Get rid of the frogs and I'll let the Israelites go!' promised Pharaoh.

Moses asked God to remove the frogs, but Pharaoh broke his promise and still wouldn't let the people go.

So God sent millions of gnats upon the land. Soon every man and beast was covered in nasty, biting insects.

'I'm still not letting them go!' said Pharaoh stubbornly.

God sent another plague. Swarms of flies covered everything. They crawled all over people's faces and covered their food like a blanket. Only the Israelites had no flies near them. It was so bad that Pharaoh again agreed to let the people go if God removed the flies.

But when all the flies were gone, Pharaoh broke his promise again. This time God sent a plague that killed all the Egyptians' cattle and other animals. Still Pharaoh was stubborn. born.

'I'm not letting a single one go!' he said.

God told Moses to take lots of ashes and throw them up into the air. Wherever the ashes landed a nasty painful sore came on the Egyptians and their animals. Even the magicians had sores all over them. But Pharaoh wouldn't change his mind.

Then the heaviest hail that the Egyptians had ever seen fell upon them. It was so bad that every man and animal outside was killed and every tree and plant flattened.

'The flax and the barley are ruined!' said Pharaoh. 'Tell your God to stop the hail before the wheat comes up and I'll let your people go!'

Moses asked God to stop the hail, but still Pharaoh refused to release the slaves. So God sent so many locusts that the skies were black with them. These enormous hungry insects ate up every plant and fruit still in Egypt, so there was nothing left to eat.

'Ask your God to forgive me and take the locusts away and I'll do what you want!' promised Pharaoh.

But, yet again, he broke his promise. God sent darkness on the land so it was pitch black for three days and nights and nobody could leave their homes.

'Get away from me with your plagues!' said Pharaoh to Moses. 'I never want to see you or your people again!'

JAKE'S STORY

Once the hailstorm was over, Father and I went to inspect the vines.

'The vines are a bit battered but the grapes seem to be fine, Jake,' said Father.

'Even losing the whole crop wouldn't be as bad as what happened to the Egyptians when their stubborn king wouldn't keep his promise,' I said.

25
Death Passes Over

God had sent terrible plagues over Egypt, but no matter what happened, Pharaoh refused to release the Israelites from slavery in his country. Before Moses had seen Pharaoh for the last time, God told him that he was going to send one more plague. Moses told Pharaoh about it before he left.

'God will pass through Egypt at midnight and every first-born male will be killed. The air will be filled with the cries and tears of sorrowful parents. Only the Hebrew people will be spared. Then you will come and *beg* me to take my people and leave!'

Moses angrily left Pharaoh and went back to his people to tell them what to do so they could be safe when death came to Egypt.

'Every family is to choose a fine lamb and kill it this evening,' he said. 'Then use its blood to paint along the doorposts outside your house. Nobody must leave their house tonight! Stay safely indoors and keep the door tightly shut while God passes through the land. When he sees the blood he will pass over your houses and not let anything hurt you.

'You must eat the lamb roasted; have your coats and sandals on, so you are ready to leave. Then you must remember this Passover by doing the same thing every year to remind yourselves and your children how God spared his people while the Egyptians were killed.'

So the people did exactly as Moses had told them. That night every Egyptian household lost their eldest son, as well as the first born of all the animals. But the Hebrew people stayed safe. Pharaoh sent messengers to Moses and begged him to leave.

In the early morning light the Hebrew slaves left Egypt at last. Six hundred thousand men took their families and their flocks and all their possessions and set off into the desert. They were free at last.

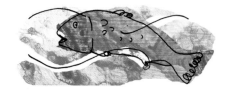

KOZ'S STORY

My name is Koz and I am the son of a fisherman on the Sea of Galilee. I spend hours and hours on the fishing boat with my father. I often wonder what's down at the bottom of the sea. The Israelites saw the bottom of the Red Sea when Moses parted the waves to let them cross safely. The Egyptians would have seen it too. But they never got to tell anyone about it, because they were washed away and drowned!

26
Parting the Red Sea

God led the Israelites through the wilderness towards the Red Sea. He went with them in a pillar of cloud in the daytime and a pillar of flames at night. These pillars moved ahead of them so that they always knew which way to go.

Back in Egypt, Pharaoh was very angry at the loss of all his slaves.

'I need those Hebrews to work for me!' he said. 'Get the whole army ready! We'll capture them and bring them back!'

So the Egyptian army set off to chase after the Israelites, who were camped by the water. When they saw the huge cloud of dust raised by more than six hundred chariots, the Israelites knew that Pharaoh was after them. They were terrified and turned to Moses in anger.

'Why did you bring us out here?' they wailed. 'It would have been better to stay and live as slaves than to be killed out here in this awful desert!'

'Don't be frightened', said Moses. 'God will save us all and destroy the Egyptian army!'

'Point your rod over the sea', said God to Moses. 'I will push back the sea so that my people can cross in safety.'

So Moses held his big staff out over the raging sea. Immediately the water was divided by a strong east wind, leaving a dry path down the middle for the people to cross. The huge pillar of cloud went behind them now, so that the Egyptians couldn't see them.

But soon the Egyptian army found the dry path and followed them, getting closer every minute. By the time the last of the Israelites had safely crossed the sea, the fast horses of the Egyptian chariots had almost caught up with them.

God told Moses to raise his rod over the sea once more. As he did so, the huge walls of water tumbled down upon the charging Egyptians like a giant tidal wave. Every single one of them was drowned.

Moses and his people were so thankful to be saved that they sang joyfully and danced in celebration, before setting out on their journey once more.

MARA'S STORY

My name is Mara and I help my mother make butter. First I heat milk in a pottery churn. Then I add sour goat's milk and stir vigorously. Butter making is hard work but I always think how good the bread and butter will taste when it's made. It reminds me of a story about the days when the Israelites didn't have anything to eat, so God sent food from heaven.

27
Food from Heaven

God rescued the fleeing Israelites by parting the Red Sea so they could cross. Although they were now safe from the Egyptian army their struggles were far from over. After a few weeks in the desert the Israelites started complaining to Moses.

'At least we had enough to eat in Egypt! Why did you bring us here to starve?'

'God will look after you even though you complain so much,' said Moses. 'God will send us food from heaven. There will be meat to eat tonight, and tomorrow we will find bread.'

Later that evening, thousands of quails flew down. The people caught the little birds, cooked them and ate until they were full. Next morning the Israelites found a special food called 'manna' on the ground. The people had never seen the white flakes before and didn't know what they were.

'Eat it, it's delicious!' said Moses. 'But don't gather more than you need for today or it will go rotten. Only on the day before the Sabbath can you gather twice as much, so you won't have to work that day.'

All the time the Israelites were in the desert God sent them quails and manna every day, so they never went hungry. But sometimes there was no water to drink and the people got angry with Moses again.

God told him to hit a big rock with his staff. When Moses did so, water gushed from the rock like a stream. So, despite their complaints, God made sure that his people always had enough food and drink.

LEVI'S STORY

I am Levi, a donkey boy, and I work for Balaam, who is an important man, a prophet. Even the king listens to him, because God speaks directly to Balaam. My favourite donkey is called Judy and I'd just brought food for her.

'Here's some fresh hay, Judy,' I said. 'How are you feeling today?'

I listened hard, but the donkey made no reply. I sighed. I'd been trying to encourage her to talk to me for months but I'd not heard a single word since the day my master told me to saddle up Judy to take him to visit King Balak. The king wanted Balaam to ask God to send great evil to hurt the Israelites. But God used an amazing miracle to show Balaam what to do.

The Amazing 28 Talking Donkey

The Israelites camped near the land of King Balak, in Moab. Balak was terrified that such a huge number of Israelites would take over his land so he asked Balaam to curse them. Balaam asked God about it many times, but God always told him not to do it.

But Balaam loved money, so he was excited when at last God said to him, 'Go then, but say exactly what I tell you.' They were riding along, when suddenly his donkey stood still. She could see an angel holding a sword in front of them. Frightened, she turned off into a field.

As Balaam hit the donkey and pulled her back on to the road, the angel moved further down. When the donkey tried to squirm past the angel by pressing hard against the wall, Balaam's foot got crushed against the hard stones. He roared with rage, beating her hard.

They came to a narrow place where they couldn't pass the angel, so Balaam's donkey lay down in the road. He was furious and beat her even harder.

Then God made the animal talk like a person.

'Why have you beaten me three times?'

Furiously, Balaam replied, 'You're making a fool of me! I should kill you!'

'Do I usually behave like this?' asked the donkey.

'Well . . . no,' admitted Balaam.

Then God opened Balaam's eyes to what the donkey had seen all along. Balaam fell down on his knees before the angel standing in the road with his drawn sword.

'Why have you beaten your donkey three times?' asked the angel. 'If she hadn't got out of my way I would have killed you with my sword and saved her life.'

'Forgive me! I was greedy for money,' moaned Balaam. 'Shall I go home now?'

'No, go to King Balak. But say only what God tells you,' said the angel.

When Balaam met King Balak, he refused to curse the Israelites. Three times, King Balak tried to persuade Balaam, offering him more and more rewards. But Balaam blessed them instead. King Balak was very angry.

'I could make you rich, but your God has kept you from that! Get out of here! I never want to see you again!'

So Balaam and his donkey returned home safely.

TAMAR'S STORY

My name is Tamar and I'm the daughter of a flax spinner. There is a lot of work to do before the flax is ready for spinning and my sisters and I try to help. Mother put down the large wooden club she used for pounding the wet flax and rubbed her sore back. It was hard work separating the fibres from the stalk.

'I've already taken down the dry flax from the roof,' she said. 'I'll start spinning that now and soon there'll be a big batch to take to the weavers. Now, please will you girls take all this flax up on to the roof and spread it to dry?'

My sisters and I climbed up with our bundles of soggy flax. As we spread out the wet fibres on our big flat roof I remembered a story about someone who hid something dangerous under the flax on her roof.

29
Rahab and the Spies

Moses lived to be very old and after he died God made Joshua the leader of the Israelites. Joshua sent two men to spy out the Promised Land. The spies went to the city of Jericho and stayed at the house of a woman called Rahab. But the king heard about the Hebrew spies and sent soldiers to Rahab's house to capture them.

'Two men were here earlier,' said Rahab, when the soldiers came. 'But they've left now. You'd better chase them quickly, or you won't be able to catch them!'

When the soldiers had left she climbed up on to her flat roof where drying flax was laid out in neat rows.

'You can come out now,' she whispered. 'The soldiers have gone.'

The two spies crawled out from under the flax.

'The whole country is scared of you Israelites,' said Rahab. 'We heard how your God even parted the Red Sea for you when you came out of Egypt. He must be a very great God! Promise me that you will not kill my family when you take over our city!'

'Don't worry,' said the spies. 'You saved us, so we'll save you. Bring all your relatives here to stay. Then hang a scarlet cord from the window so our men know not to attack your house.'

It was late and the gates of the city had been locked, so the spies couldn't walk out. But Rahab's house was built into the city wall. So they climbed down a rope from her window and escaped safely.

JESSE'S STORY

I am called Jesse and my father makes trumpets for the priests. He is very pleased today because he has two new sons, but my brother Sol and I are not so sure.

'What an awful noise!' grumbled Sol, and put his fingers in his ears. I did the same, but it didn't help much. We could still hear our new twins screaming their heads off.

'You and Jesse were just as bad when you were babies,' said Father, as he polished a ram's horn to make it into a trumpet. 'The whole family would have made good members of Joshua's army!'

'Whose army?' asked Sol.

'Joshua's army used horns like this to capture a city,' I explained. 'The priests made them into trumpets called shofars.'

30
Walls Come Tumbling Down

Joshua and his army had surrounded the city of Jericho, ready to capture it. God told Joshua what to do.

'Every day for the next seven days I want you to march your army round the city. Behind the soldiers put seven priests carrying trumpets. At the end of the week you will all march round seven times with the priests blowing on their *shofars*. At the last blast from the trumpets I want all the army to shout as loudly as they can. Then the walls of the city will collapse and you can capture it easily.'

Joshua told the army exactly what to do. For six days they all marched silently round the city. The people of Jericho watched this strange procession in disbelief. They wondered how Joshua's army could possibly capture their city this way, but they did not know about God's promise.

Then on the seventh day Joshua said, 'God will give us this city if we shout with all our strength. Remember not to kill Rahab and her family in the house with the scarlet cord hanging from the window. Do not steal anything for yourselves, but bring everything valuable you capture back to me for God's treasury.'

So for the seventh time the army marched round the city, the trumpets sounded, and the men yelled with all their might. The walls of Jericho came tumbling down and it was easy for the army to leap over all the rubble and capture the city. But they spared Rahab, who had believed that their God was the true god.

The Israelites had begun to capture the Promised Land.

JESSE'S STORY

My father makes fine trumpets and when I grow up I'd like to play one of his trumpets in a battle, like the priests used to do. I know another good story about trumpets in battle.

31
Gideon Puts Out a Fleece

After Joshua died the Israelites were without a leader. Midian was the land east of the Red Sea and for seven years the Midianites ruled the Israelites. They stole their grain and animals so the Israelites had to hide in caves to escape them. An angel came to a man called Gideon with a message from God.

'I have chosen you to save Israel,' said God. 'You will be a mighty warrior.'

Gideon was shocked. 'My tribe is the smallest,' he said, 'and I'm the least important person in it! Why pick me?'

'With you as leader, the Israelites will defeat the Midianites,' promised God.

Gideon called all the other tribes to help him in the battle. But he was still worried, so he prayed to God.

'I'll put out a woollen fleece tonight,' Gideon said. 'If the fleece is wet tomorrow morning and the floor around it is dry, I'll know you mean what you say.'

Next morning the fleece was soaking wet and the floor dry, but Gideon was still nervous.

'I'll put out the fleece again tonight, Lord. If it stays dry while the floor becomes wet, I'll know for *sure* that you want me to save Israel.'

Sure enough, the fleece stayed dry, so Gideon prepared for battle.

Gideon had more than thirty thousand men ready when God said to him, 'With this many men they will think it is their own bravery that makes you win, not the help of God. Send most of them home!'

So Gideon was left with only three hundred men to fight against the huge Midianite army. He gave each man a torch, a jar and a trumpet. The men carried the burning torches in the pottery jars, so their enemies couldn't see the flames.

'Creep up on our enemies silently while they are sleeping,' ordered Gideon. 'When I give the word, smash the jars and wave your flaming torches, blow your trumpets and yell, "For the Lord and Gideon!" and we'll be sure to win!'

When the Midianites woke up and heard the shrieking of the *shofars*, and the yells of the men and saw the flaming torches they panicked, because they thought they were surrounded. They ran away, even attacking each other in their confusion. Gideon and his small band of Israelites had won the battle with the help of God.

TIMNA'S STORY

I'm Timna, and my mother is a sweet maker in the town of Nain. I love watching her making the delicious sweets, but I love eating them even more.

'I'm ready to add the honey to the cakes now,' said Mother.

'I'll get it!' I said, carefully carrying the heavy pot across the room.

'You must be as strong as Samson to carry that heavy pot!' Mother said admiringly.

As she poured in the pure syrup I remembered the amazing story of Samson, the strong man.

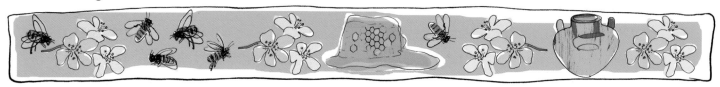

32
Samson and Delilah

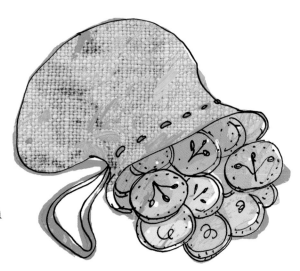

When Samson was born, God told his parents that his hair must never be cut because he would be a special man, who would help the Israelites against their enemies, the Philistines.

Samson grew up to be so strong that one day he ripped a wild lion apart with his bare hands. He killed a thousand of his enemies with the jawbone of an ass. This made the Philistines terrified of him.

Then he fell in love with a woman called Delilah. The Philistines offered to pay Delilah eleven hundred pieces of silver if she would find out the secret of Samson's strength.

'You are so strong!' she said to Samson. 'How could anyone overpower you?'

Samson told her that being tied up with fresh bowstrings would take away his strength. Then he told her that tying him up with new ropes or plaiting his hair would take away his strength. But each time Samson broke free easily.

Delilah kept pestering Samson to tell her his secret, but each time he fooled her.

'Why won't you tell me the secret of your strength?' cried Delilah. 'If you *really* loved me you wouldn't tease me like this!'

So Samson told her the secret.

Immediately Delilah told the Philistines and that night they crept in and shaved off all Samson's hair while he was asleep. When Delilah woke him up he could not fight the Philistines because his hair had kept him strong and now it was gone. He was captured, blinded and put in prison.

Much later, the Philistine rulers were having a feast with thousands of people in their temple. They remembered Samson and had him brought out of prison to entertain them.

Samson prayed to God.

'Make me strong again so I can kill these Philistines who blinded me. Then I will die happy.'

Samson's hair had grown long again while he was in prison. He was standing between two stone pillars, which he pushed apart with his strong arms. They crashed to the floor, bringing the roof falling down and killing everyone in the temple, including Samson. He killed more of his enemies with this one act than he had in the whole of his life.

SARAH'S STORY

My name is Sarah and my father is a farmer in the Jordan valley. My father always leaves a strip of barley unharvested at the edge of his fields. It is the law and it is also the only way that poor people like widows and orphans can find any food to eat. I know a story about a widow called Naomi.

33
Ruth and Naomi

Naomi was an Israelite, but she lived in Moab with her husband, her two sons and their wives. When her husband and sons died she decided to travel back to her home village of Bethlehem. But Ruth, one of her daughters-in-law, loved her dearly and didn't want to leave her.

'I will come with you,' said Ruth. 'Your land will be my land and your God will be my God.'

So they went to
Bethlehem, but as
they didn't have any
way of getting food
Ruth went to glean in
the fields of Boaz, a relative
of Naomi. She was picking
up leftover grain for them to
eat when Boaz found out who she was. He
told her to stay with his servants and take
as much grain as she wanted.

'Why are you so kind to me?' she asked.

'I've been told how good you've been to Naomi,' he said. 'You left your
own country and came here to live with foreigners, just to look after her.'

Naomi was thrilled when she heard that Ruth had got on so well
with Boaz. She told Ruth to put on her best clothes and go to visit
Boaz at night. Ruth went and lay at his feet as he slept.

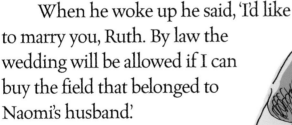

When he woke up he said, 'I'd like
to marry you, Ruth. By law the
wedding will be allowed if I can
buy the field that belonged to
Naomi's husband.'

So Boaz arranged to
buy the field and soon he
and Ruth were happily
married. Naomi was so
thrilled when a little
grandson was born,
that she praised God
for his goodness.

LEAH'S STORY

My name is Leah and my family keeps goats to make cheese that we sell in the market-place. I'm the oldest girl in the family so I help by looking after the little ones. There always seem to be a couple of toddlers in our house and I enjoy playing with them. But what I really love is to hold a new baby in my arms and rock it to sleep. It must be so sad not to have any children at all! I hope I have lots when I grow up. I know a story about someone who wanted a baby very badly.

34
Hannah Keeps her Promise

Hannah longed for children of her own. Her husband Elkanah had another wife, Peninnah, as was the custom in their country, and they had children. Peninnah was horrible to Hannah and always made fun of her.

Every year they journeyed to the temple at Shiloh, to worship and make sacrifices to God. Peninnah teased Hannah all the way, making her cry so much she couldn't eat. Elkanah tried to cheer her up, because he really loved Hannah, but she was not comforted.

One evening Hannah returned to the temple and wept bitterly as she prayed silently to God.

'Please, God, if you will give me a son, I promise I'll let him serve in your temple for the whole of his life.'

Hannah's lips moved silently as she prayed. Eli, the priest, saw this and thought she was drunk. He was very angry.

'You cannot come to God's house in a drunken state!' he shouted.

'I'm not drunk!' said Hannah. 'I'm just so very sad. I was telling God my troubles and asking him to help me.'

'In that case, may God grant your wish,' replied the priest.

Hannah was filled with hope at Eli's words. In time, God answered her prayers and gave her a fine son.

'I asked God for him, so I'll call him Samuel,' she said happily, 'because Samuel means "asked of God".'

When Samuel was big enough to eat proper food and run about the house, Hannah took him back to the temple.

'Do you remember me?' she asked Eli. 'A few years ago you saw me praying silently to God. He has answered my prayer and given me this beautiful son, Samuel. Now I want to fulfil my promise. I am giving my son back to God, so that he may serve him in the temple all his life.'

Eli praised God for Hannah's faithfulness and took Samuel in to learn to help in the temple. Every year Hannah visited Samuel and brought a new little coat that she had sewn especially for him.

ABIMELECH'S STORY

My name's Abimelech, but my friend Samuel calls me Bim. I've just come here to work in the temple, which is God's house, where people come to worship him. Samuel's been working with Eli, the chief priest, since he was a tiny boy. Samuel's just told me the weirdest story, so I'll tell you and see if you think God's got a special job ahead for him.

35
The Voice in the Night

Poor old Eli the priest is nearly blind now. His sons are really evil men and don't love or serve God. Samuel was sleeping, but woke up when he heard someone calling him. He knew it must be Eli, so he ran down to his room.

'Here I am!' Samuel yawned. 'What do you want?'

'Nothing, Samuel!' said Eli. 'I never called you!'

Three times he heard the call, but he wasn't wanted.

The third time Samuel said, 'I definitely heard you calling my name, Eli!'

Eli sat up in bed and got very excited.

'Messages from God are very rare in these sad times, Samuel,' he said. 'But I'm sure it's him calling your name! He must have an important message for us!

76

'Go back to bed. If he calls your name, you must say, "Speak, Lord. Your servant is listening." '

Samuel went slowly back to bed. Why should God choose a small boy like him to talk to? A few minutes later he heard God call.

'Samuel! Samuel!'

'Speak, Lord. Your servant is listening', he whispered, very scared.

'I have warned Eli that I would judge his whole family if he didn't stop his sons behaving in the wicked way they do. But he has done nothing to stop them, so I have decided they will all be punished.'

It was an important message from God to Eli. But why tell Samuel, who was too scared to say anything? He pulled the bedcovers over his head and stayed there, shivering, until morning. But then he had to get up and open the doors of the temple so the people could get in to worship. He rushed round the temple, doing his jobs and trying to avoid Eli. But it wasn't long before Eli caught up with Samuel.

'Tell me exactly what God said to you last night!'

So Samuel had to tell him about God's punishment. Eli sighed deeply and said, 'He is God. He must do what he thinks is right. God is blessing your work here, Samuel. I think he wants you to be a prophet, a man who speaks God's words to his people.'

JOEL'S STORY

My name is Joel and I'm the son of an olive grower. One day when I was walking through my father's olive grove I heard the sound of loud crying. It was a boy, his fists pressed into his eyes and tears pouring down his cheeks.

'Whatever's the matter?' I asked.

'My donkey ran away!' he wailed.

'I'll help you find him,' I said.

As we searched for the donkey I remembered a story I'd heard. It was about a handsome young man, taller than anyone else, who heard some amazing news while he was looking for his lost donkeys.

36
Saul for King

Samuel was a good man and the people listened to him. When he was old he made his sons judges, but they were bad men and the people didn't want them.

'We want a king like all the other countries!' they said.

'A king will make you obey him and give him most of your possessions,' warned Samuel. 'Then you'll wish you'd never asked for one.'

But the people insisted, so Samuel asked God to help him choose a king. Next day Samuel met a young man called Saul.

'I've been searching for my donkeys for three days,' said Saul. 'They say you are a man of God. Can you tell me where they are?'

'Your donkeys have been found,' said Samuel. 'Come and eat with me and I will tell you what God has chosen for you.'

After their meal Samuel poured some holy oil on Saul's head to show that God had a special job for him to do.

'God has chosen you to be king,' said Samuel. 'I've called all the Israelites together next week. Make sure you come to the meeting so that I can tell them about you.'

But when the time came for the meeting, Saul was nowhere to be seen. He was so scared of being chosen king that he had hidden among the tents and baggage that all the people had brought. But someone found him and brought him out to show the people.

'Here is your king!' said Samuel.

The people saw how tall and handsome Saul was and began to shout and cheer. 'Long live the king!' they shouted.

JOEL'S STORY

We found the lost donkey trying to nibble the leaves of one of the young olive trees.

'Don't eat that!' I yelled, grabbing the donkey's rope and pulling it away from the tree. 'That's my tree! My father planted it for me when I was born.'

'It's not a very good tree,' said the boy. 'It doesn't even have any olives!'

'Olive trees don't have any fruit for the first fifteen years,' I said. 'But they will be the best olives in the world. The priests mix the olive oil with cinnamon, cassia and myrrh to make a special anointing oil that they use to anoint a new king.'

37
From Shepherd Boy to King

Saul was king for a long time, but he disobeyed God, who decided to choose a new king. Samuel was upset about this, but God said to him, 'Fill up your ram's horn with anointing oil and go to Bethlehem. I'm going to make one of Jesse's sons king.'

So Samuel went to Bethlehem, where Jesse lived, and asked to see his sons. The eldest son, Eliab, was big and strong and Samuel thought that he must be the one God had chosen. But God said to him, 'I am not like ordinary people who only look at the outside of a person. What they are like inside is much more important. That's what I look at!'

Samuel looked at all seven of Jesse's sons, who were all fine men, but Samuel knew that none of them was God's chosen king.

'Do you have any other sons?' he asked.

'Only my youngest boy, David,' said Jesse. 'He's out looking after the sheep.'

Samuel asked Jesse to fetch David. When he came in, Samuel saw he was strong and bright-eyed.

'This is the one,' God said to Samuel. 'Anoint David with oil. I have chosen him to be the new King of Israel.'

So Samuel poured the holy oil on the shepherd boy and David was filled with the Holy Spirit.

MILCAH'S STORY

My name is Milcah and my brother is a shepherd boy. Tonight will be the first night he's spent with the flock out on the hills. He's watching me impatiently as I make him a new sling. He'll need it in case lions or bears come and try to steal the sheep.

'Don't worry about tonight, Jemuel!' I said, as I finished sewing. 'This is a very strong sling and you're a good shot, like another shepherd boy called David.'

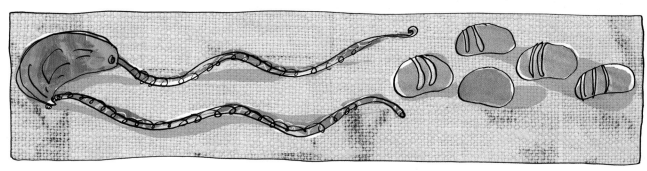

38
David and Goliath

The armies of Israel and their enemies, the Philistines, were at war. For forty days Goliath, the biggest man in the Philistine army, stood and roared at the Israelites.

'Choose one man to come and fight me. If he beats me, then all of us will be your slaves, but if I win, you will be ours!'

Everyone was scared to death, because Goliath was nearly ten feet tall. He wore a bronze helmet and strong armour and nobody was brave enough to fight him.

One day David came to bring his brothers some food, because they were in the Israelite army. He heard Goliath and was amazed and angry that nobody would fight him. When Saul saw him, David immediately told him that *he* would fight Goliath.

'But you're just a boy!' said Saul. 'How can you fight such a giant?'

'I'm a shepherd boy,' said David. 'Every day I have to defend my flocks against lions and bears. God saves me from wild animals, so I know he can save me from this giant Philistine!'

'Go then, and may God be with you!' said Saul.

He gave David his armour and the boy tried it on, but it was much too big and heavy.

'I'll go just as I am,' said David, taking it off.

He went down to the stream and chose five smooth round stones. Then he walked out to where Goliath stood.

'Why have they sent a mere boy to fight me?' Goliath roared. 'I will kill him and feed him to the birds!'

'You come to fight with a sword, a spear and a javelin and hope to kill me!' said David. 'But I come in the name of the Lord God of Israel. He will make sure I kill you and then everyone will know that this victory belongs to God!'

David raced towards Goliath, swinging his sling above his head. The stone hit Goliath in the middle of his forehead and he dropped down dead. David ran and cut Goliath's head off with the giant's own sword.

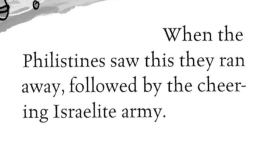

When the Philistines saw this they ran away, followed by the cheering Israelite army.

DINAH'S STORY

My name is Dinah and my father is a horse trader. I've just become an older sister because my mother had twin boys last week. A few days later my aunt had a baby boy too, so our house is full of babies! I can't really tell them apart, but Mother and Aunt know exactly which one is which. They say that mothers can always tell their own baby. Aunt told me the story of wise King Solomon, who had to decide which baby was which, years ago. Do you know that story?

39
Wise King Solomon

David, the shepherd boy, became king and reigned for forty years. He made a lot of mistakes, but he was usually a good king. He loved music and wrote many songs of praise to God. When David was very old and frail he made his son Solomon king. One night God appeared to Solomon in a dream and offered him whatever he wanted.

'I want to be a good king, but I'm still young,' said Solomon. 'So could you please give me wisdom so I can rule your people well?'

God was pleased with this request.

'I will grant your wish,' he said, 'and because you weren't selfish when I offered you whatever you wanted, I will make you very rich and powerful too.'

Soon Solomon had to make use of his new wisdom when two women brought a baby to the king.

'We both live in the same house,' said the first woman. 'I had a baby boy recently and three days later this woman also had a son. But last night she rolled over on her baby while she was asleep and killed it. Then she took my son and put her dead baby in his place! Now she won't give him back!'

'It's not true!' said the second woman. 'It's your boy that's dead! You can't prove anything!'

Then the women began to argue and fight over the baby. King Solomon considered the problem until he had a way to find out which was the real mother.

'Be quiet!' he ordered them. 'Bring me a sword. As you can't agree whose son it really is, I shall cut the baby in two and you shall have half each!'

'All right then,' said the second woman. 'She shan't have him, so just cut him in two!'

'No, don't kill him!' begged the first woman. 'Give him to the other woman if you must, but don't kill him!'

Then King Solomon knew who the real mother was.

'Don't cut the baby in two,' he ordered. 'Give it to the first woman, because only a real mother would behave as she did.'

When the people heard of this clever way of solving the problem, they knew that wise King Solomon was truly guided by God.

LABAN'S STORY

My name is Laban and my father is a tanner in the village of Zarephath, where we live. It hasn't rained here for a very long time and everyone is praying for a miracle. But I'm sure the rain will come again, because we all believe in miracles here. I saw one happen to my best friend, Obed, who lives next door to me. It's an amazing story!

40
Elijah Saves the Widow's Son

God told Elijah the prophet to hide in a barren wilderness. There was nothing for him to eat, so every morning and night God sent down ravens with bread and meat for him. Elijah could drink from the stream, so he had everything he needed.

Then the stream dried up. God said to Elijah, 'Go to Zarephath, where I have asked a widow to give you food.'

When Elijah got to our village he found a woman and asked her for a drink of water. 'Please could I have some bread too? I'm very hungry.'

'I don't have any bread,' the woman said sadly. 'I've only got a handful of flour at home, and a little bit of oil. I'm just gathering some firewood to cook this last meal for my son and me. Then I'm sure we'll starve to death.'

'Don't worry,' said Elijah. 'Go home and cook the meal you planned. But first make me a little loaf of bread. God promises that neither your flour nor your oil will run out until rain falls again on the crops of Israel.'

The woman did exactly as Elijah had asked and God did what he promised. There was always flour in the crock and oil in the jar, no matter how much they used. Every day they had enough food to eat.

Then the widow's young son became very ill and died.

'Are you punishing me for my sins by killing my son?' the widow asked him, as she wept over the body.

'Give him to me!' said Elijah.

He carried the boy upstairs to his own room, where it was cooler, and laid him on the bed. Then he cried out to God, 'Why have you brought this sadness to the widow who has been so kind to me?'

He stretched his arms over the boy three times and prayed, 'O God, please return this child's life to him!'

God heard Elijah's prayer and the boy came back to life, so he took him back downstairs to his mother. The widow was so happy and thanked Elijah.

'Now I know for sure that you are a man of God and whatever you say comes from him!' she said.

LILAH'S STORY

My name is Lilah and I am an orphan. I survive by gathering wood in the hills. There are always bands of travellers passing by. They stop in our small village to rest their animals and make a meal each evening. I bring them wood and start their fire for them and then they share their food with me. They let me sit by the fire and listen to their stories too and that's often even better than the food.

It's easy to get a fire going with dry wood, but every time the wood is damp I remember the story of how the prophet Elijah started a blazing fire with wood that was very wet. I wish I'd been there to see it.

41
Fire from Heaven

After three years without rain God sent Elijah to tell wicked King Ahab that the drought and famine in his country was going to end. 'Not you again, you troublemaker!' said Ahab when he saw Elijah.

'It's you and your family who make trouble for Israel by worshipping the idol, Baal, instead of God', said Elijah. 'Now bring all the people and the prophets of Baal to Mount Carmel.'

When everyone was gathered on the mountain Elijah said, 'It's time for you all to decide who to follow. We'll have a contest between me and the four hundred and fifty prophets of Baal.

'We'll sacrifice bulls and make altars to burn them on. Then we will call upon our gods. Whichever one sends fire from heaven will be the true God.'

So the prophets of Baal prepared their sacrifice and put the meat on the altar. They danced around it and called out to Baal for fire.

'Perhaps Baal is asleep!' said Elijah, when nothing had happened by midday.

By nighttime there was still no fire. Then Elijah called the people to watch him. He built an altar, put twelve big stones around it and dug a large trench around the altar.

'Bring four big pots of water and pour them on my altar!' he said.

The people poured the water on the altar so the wood and meat were soon soaking wet. Three times they refilled the pots until even the trench was full of water.

'Show the people that you are the true God and I am your servant!' Elijah prayed. 'Show them your power so they will return to you!'

Then God sent fire blazing down from heaven. It was so fierce that it burnt up all the wet wood, the meat and even the stones and licked up all the water in the trench.

Then the people believed in God again and called out, 'The Lord is the true God!'

ABE'S STORY

My name is Abe and I am the son of a chariot maker in the town of Bethel. All day I work in the smithy by the hot fire, helping my father shape iron chariots. The metal glows brightly in the light from the fire and reminds me of the story of the prophet Elijah being taken up into heaven in a chariot of fire.

42
Chariot of Fire

After many years serving God on earth, it was time for Elijah to be taken up to heaven. Another prophet, Elisha, was going to carry on his work, but he was sad to see Elijah go.

'I'm going to Bethel now,' said Elijah. 'Why don't you wait here?'

'No, I'm coming with you,' said Elisha.

When they got to Bethel the people said to Elisha, 'Don't you know that God's going to take Elijah soon?'

'Don't remind me!' said Elisha sadly.

'I'm going to Jericho next,' said Elijah. 'Why don't you stay here, Elisha?'

'Wherever you go, I'm coming with you,' said Elisha firmly and went with him to Jericho and then to the River Jordan. Here Elijah rolled up his cloak and hit the water with it. The waters divided, so they could cross to the other side.

'The time has
come for me to go,'
said Elijah. 'Is there
anything I can do for
you before I go?'

'I'm going to need
a double measure of your
spirit to do your job,' said Elisha.
'Could you give me that?'

'That's a hard one!' said Elijah. 'If you see me go, you
will know you have your wish. If you don't see me, you will not have it.'

A chariot and horses of fire appeared as he spoke and Elisha
watched in awe as Elijah was carried up to heaven in a
whirlwind.

Elisha was very sad to see him go. He picked up Elijah's cloak and walked back to the river. He hit the water
with the cloak and the waters parted for him, just as
they had done for Elijah. He crossed the river
to where the prophets of Jordan were waiting.
They had seen everything and said to
Elisha, 'The spirit of Elijah has
come upon you!'

So Elisha knew that
his last request had
been granted.

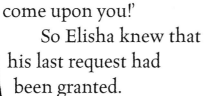

SETH'S STORY

I'm Seth and I'm a fisherman's son. When the wheat is ripe, I sneeze. When I walk through a flower-filled meadow, I sneeze. Sometimes I sneeze so many times I think my head will fall off! I'm glad I'm not a farmer's son. Out here on the lake there's nothing to make me sneeze. Instead I can think about all the stories my family tell, while we wait for the fish to swim into our nets. One of my favourites is about a rich woman's son who once sneezed seven times in a row.

43
Seven Sneezes

Elisha was often invited to eat at the home of a rich lady in Shunem. One day she said to her husband, 'Let's build an extra room on to our house, then Elisha can stay there whenever he comes to Shunem.'

Elisha visited often and was pleased at her kindness. One day he said to his servant Gehazi, 'What can I do for this good lady who has been so kind?'

'She has no son,' said Gehazi, 'and her husband is quite old.'

So Elisha said to the woman, 'This time next year when I visit, you'll have a baby son in your arms.'

The woman couldn't believe it and thought Elisha was teasing her. But within a year she was filled with joy when she gave birth to a boy, just as Elisha had told her. The boy grew to be strong and helped his father in the fields. But one day the boy had terrible pains in his head and after a few hours he died.

The rich woman laid him on Elisha's bed and rushed off to Mount Carmel to tell the prophet what had happened. He came back with her, but sent Gehazi on ahead, giving him his staff and telling him to lay it on the boy. Gehazi raced to the house and laid the staff along the boy's body, but nothing happened.

Elisha went into his room alone and found the child lying there, cold and dead. He prayed to God, then stretched his arms over the boy until he felt him begin to get warm.

He did this several times, until the boy sneezed seven times and opened his eyes. Elisha called for the child's mother, who was filled with joy as she rushed in and hugged her son.

ABNER'S STORY

My name is Abner and I work as a goatherd in the hills of Babylon. My goats are the stupidest in the world! They keep wandering into this valley looking for food and I hate going after them because there's nothing here but bones. It's a bit scary really, but I'm the youngest, so I always get sent to find them. As I stopped to rub my sore knees I saw a very strange sight. A man suddenly appeared out of nowhere. I've seen him in the village so I recognised him as Ezekiel, the priest. But how could he have just flown out of the sky like an eagle?

44
Rattling Bones

Ezekiel was a prophet who worked with the Israelites who were exiled into the foreign land of Babylon. God set Ezekiel down in the valley and showed him the dry heaps of bones.

'These aren't old animal bones!' said Ezekiel in surprise. 'They're people's skeletons! This valley is a gigantic graveyard.'

'Could these bones become alive again?' God asked him.

Ezekiel had never heard of skeletons becoming alive!

'Tell these bones that I'm going to give them muscles,

cover them with skin and make them live and breathe once more. Then they will know for sure just how powerful I am', said God.

So Ezekiel repeated God's words. Hardly had he finished speaking when there was a loud rattling noise. The bones of each body rattled together as they attached themselves exactly as they used to be. Soon the bones were covered with muscles and skin and looked like real people again.

'Now I want you to call the winds, Ezekiel', said God. 'Tell them to blow from every corner of the earth and breathe life into these dead bodies'.

Ezekiel ordered the winds to blow and immediately the bodies become real live men again. There were so many of them that they looked like a huge army stretching right across the valley.

Then God told Ezekiel what this meant. 'These bones stand for the people of Israel', he said. 'They live in a foreign land, as miserable and without hope as a heap of dried-up old bones. But I will breathe new life into them just as I have into these dry bones. I will bring them home and look after them. They will become powerful again and live in peace'.

ABIGAIL'S STORY

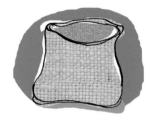

I am Abigail, a spice merchant's daughter. I love to see the bags of spices open in my father's shop. They look like a many-coloured blanket: yellow, orange and brown, black and white and lots of shades of green. I like the smells too, many so strong they make my nose tickle.

Some customers want spices already ground when they buy them, ready to flavour their food that day, and that's a job I can do. As I grind the spices, I like to remember the stories I've heard about the faraway places some spices come from, or people who depended on them. Best of all I like the stories of Daniel, who was captured by the Babylonian king, Nebuchadnezzar.

45
Vegetables *are* Good for You!

When the Babylonians captured Jerusalem, they took captives back to Babylon. They chose the strongest and cleverest young Israelites to train them to work in the King's palace. Daniel and three of his friends were captured and were told they would spend three years learning to speak and write in the language of the Babylonians.

Daniel didn't mind this so much, but he didn't want to eat the same rich food the king did, or drink lots of wine. He knew that it wasn't healthy and it also contained foods forbidden by his faith.

'My friends and I don't want to eat your rich food, or drink wine,' said Daniel. 'We'd like a much plainer diet. Lentils and vegetables flavoured with the spice cumin, or garlic, would be excellent. And we just want water to drink.'

'I can't do that!' said the guard. 'The king wants to fatten you up and has ordered you to eat his food. If I just gave you vegetables and water you'd grow weak and probably die. Then the king would blame me and he'd definitely kill me!'

'Vegetables are *very* healthy,' said Daniel. 'Let us eat them for ten days. We could hardly die in such a short time! Then you'll see I'm right.'

So the guard let them try their new diet. After ten days they were fitter and healthier than the others who had eaten the rich food and wine. So they were allowed to eat what they wanted.

The three years passed and God gave Daniel the gift of wisdom and understanding dreams. King Nebuchadnezzar found that Daniel was cleverer than all his magicians, so he gave Daniel an important job.

ABIGAIL'S STORY

My father has been selling spices for thirty years and he knows everything about them. He told me you should never eat strongly spiced food just before you go to bed, or you will be sure to have nightmares! I think that's why King Nebuchadnezzar had such bad dreams.

46
Nebuchadnezzar's Bad Dream

King Nebuchadnezzar kept having a horrible nightmare. He didn't know what it meant so he summoned all the wise men in Babylon to explain his dream to him.

'Tell me what my dream means!' he ordered.

'Tell us about your dream first, or how can we say what it means?' they replied.

'If you are as clever as you pretend you should know without me telling you!' he insisted. 'Tell me, or you will all die!'

'Only the gods can do such things!' they protested.

King Nebuchadnezzar was so angry he ordered all the court officials to be executed, including Daniel and his friends. When Daniel heard about this he prayed to God to save their lives by telling him the king's dream and what it meant. So God gave him all the answers.

'No man is clever enough to explain your dream,'
Daniel said to the king next day. 'But God knows
everything and he has told me that your dream is
about what will happen in the future.'

'Tell me my dream and what it means!'
ordered the king.

'You saw a huge statue of a man,' said Daniel.
'Its head was gold, its body silver and its legs were
bronze. Then a rock hit the statue's feet, which
were made of iron and clay and broke them
into many pieces. The whole statue crumbled
into millions of little bits and was blown
away by the wind. The rock became an
enormous
mountain, covering the whole world.'

'You are right,' said the king. 'But
what does it mean?'

'The gold stands for your own strong
kingdom,' said Daniel, 'the silver and bronze
for other smaller kingdoms. The rock that
destroyed everything is God's eternal kingdom. One day this will cover the whole
world.'

The king realised that Daniel must be
speaking the truth to know his dream
without ever being told.

'Your God must truly be Lord of all!' said
King Nebuchadnezzar. 'Stay here with me,
Daniel, and I will reward you and make you
ruler of all of Babylon!'

So Daniel made sure his friends
had good jobs too, but he stayed
with the king.

MEL'S STORY

My name is Mel and my father is an iron maker in the town of Bethany. Today he is making a new plough for one of the farmers nearby. He has to make the iron very hot, so it becomes soft enough to be hammered into shape. My job is to pump the bellows to make the furnace really hot. The searing heat from the furnace reminds me of the amazing story of Daniel in the fiery furnace.

47
The Fiery Furnace

King Nebuchadnezzar made a huge golden statue and commanded all his people to come and see it.

'Every time my musicians play on their instruments, you must all bow down and worship this statue!' he ordered. 'Anyone who disobeys will be thrown into a fiery furnace!'

Nebuchadnezzar had given Daniel's three friends new names. He called them Shadrach, Meshach and Abednego. They, like Daniel, were all Jews and worshipped only God, so they refused to bow down to the statue. When the king heard about this he was very angry.

'I'll give you one more chance to bow down to my statue,' he told them. 'If you don't, your God cannot save you from the fiery furnace!'

'Our God could save us from the flames if he wished. But even if he doesn't, we won't bow down to anyone but him,' they replied bravely.

King Nebuchadnezzar was so angry that he ordered the furnace to be made seven times hotter. It was so hot that the soldiers who tied up Shadrach, Meshach and Abednego and threw them into the furnace were burnt up immediately. The king expected the three friends to be burnt up too, so he was amazed to see four men walking about in the fire.

'Who is that shining creature that looks like a son of the gods?' he asked. 'And how can they be walking about when we tied them up and threw them into such hot fire?'

King Nebuchadnezzar realised that theirs must be the true God and called them out. Shadrach, Meshach and Abednego came out of the fire. Neither their clothes nor their bodies were burnt. They didn't even smell of smoke!

'Everyone must praise their God!' said Nebuchadnezzar. 'They were willing to die rather than worship another god, but their true God sent an angel to rescue them!'

Then he promoted them all to better jobs in his kingdom.

ALVAN'S STORY

My name is Alvan and I am apprenticed to a silversmith. The other boys and I watch our master closely, for we all long to be allowed to work with the precious silver. I have been apprenticed here longest and I've seen my master make the most beautiful things, like silver jewellery set with shiny blue stones. But my favourites are the cups set into the backs of silver lions or fabulous birds. I think they are as good as the cups King Belshazzar used at his feasts!

48
The Writing on the Wall

Nebuchadnezzar's son was called Belshazzar. One day, after he had become king, he was feasting with more than a thousand of his most important officials.

'Get out the sacred gold and silver cups my father stole from the temple at Jerusalem!' he commanded. 'We'll use them to drink wine.'

They drank from the precious cups and got very drunk. Then they began to worship their idols. Suddenly the king saw human fingers appear and write on the white palace wall. It was in a strange language he didn't understand, so he called his wise men to explain. But nobody could say how fingers without an arm or a body attached could write, or what the strange words meant. King Belshazzar became very frightened.

'Call Daniel', the queen advised. 'He'll know the answer.'

So the king asked Daniel to explain the strange writing. 'I'll make you the most powerful man in my kingdom if you can tell me', he said.

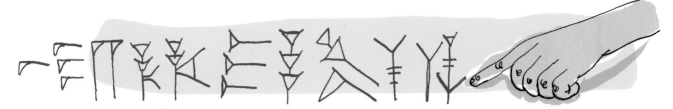

'You don't need to reward me,' said Daniel, who only wanted to serve God. 'This is the meaning of the words. God is telling you that because you used the sacred cups to drink wine at your party, you are not fit to be king. Your kingdom will be divided between the Medes and the Persians.'

Even though this was very bad news for him, Belshazzar kept his promise, and rewarded Daniel by making him a powerful leader. That same night, God's words came true when an invading army killed King Belshazzar.

ALVAN'S STORY

As I work hard polishing the silver cup my master has just made, I think about the stories of Daniel. He was so often in danger, but he always trusted in God to protect him, even when he was thrown to the lions!

49
Danger in the Lions' Den

Darius the Mede became king after Belshazzar. He liked Daniel, but everyone else was out to get him. Daniel was a good governor and King Darius wanted to put him in charge of the whole of Babylon. This made all the other officials very jealous, so they tried to get Daniel into trouble with the king. But Daniel was honest and worked very hard, so this was a hard thing for them to do.

They tricked the king into making a law that for thirty days people could pray only to the king. They knew that Daniel prayed to God every day and they wanted him to be eaten by the lions as punishment for breaking the new law.

Despite the danger he was in, Daniel prayed to God three times every day, thanking him for his goodness. The jealous officials reported him to the king, insisting that Daniel be punished by being thrown to the lions.

King Darius was horrified because he knew Daniel was a good man, but even a king could not change a law of the Medes and Persians once it was made. So Daniel was thrown into a den of hungry, vicious lions. A big stone was put in front of the lions' cave, so Daniel could not escape. All night long King Darius lay awake, worrying about Daniel and hoping that his God was strong enough to save him. Next morning he hurried to the den and called out, 'Daniel! Daniel! Did your God save you from the lions?'

'God sent an angel to stop the lions from eating me because he knew I'd done the right thing. I'm perfectly safe!' replied Daniel.

King Darius ordered that Daniel should be set free and the jealous officials thrown to the lions instead.

PEREZ'S STORY

My name is Perez and my father is a sea captain. We've spent all winter ashore, mending the sails and oars of his ship. I've been cleaning up the four heavy iron anchors and attaching new marker-buoys and now everything is shipshape. Soon the rainy season will be over and we can go to sea again. When there are lots of clouds we can't see the stars, so there's no way we can navigate. The sea's really rough in the winter too, so there's danger of shipwreck and losing all our precious cargo overboard. But at least we've never had a passenger aboard like Jonah!

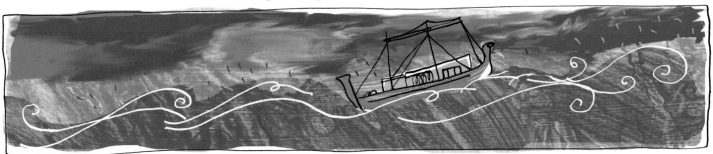

50
Jonah and the Mighty Fish

The people of Nineveh were very wicked. So God told Jonah, the prophet, to go and tell them how angry he was and order them to stop their evil ways. But Jonah was afraid to go to Nineveh because the people were so bad. Instead he bought a ticket on a ship going in the opposite direction. He hid down in the dark hold and soon went to sleep.

But God knew exactly where he was and made a huge wind blow, so that the ship was rocked by gigantic waves. The sailors were very scared. They called out to their gods for help and threw all the cargo overboard to lighten the ship. The captain was angry when he found Jonah asleep in the hold.

'How can you sleep in a storm like this!' he shouted above the roar of the sea. 'You should be praying to your God to save our lives!'

The sailors drew straws to try to see who was giving them such bad luck as to cause the storm and discovered it was Jonah.

'Who are you and what have you done to bring this great storm upon us?' they asked.

'I'm a Jew and I'm running away from my God,' admitted Jonah. 'The storm is all my fault, so the only way to stop it is to throw me overboard!'

The sailors didn't want Jonah to die, so they tried harder to row the boat ashore, but the storm just got worse and they couldn't make it. So, reluctantly, they threw him overboard, knowing he would probably drown.

The storm stopped immediately and the sailors promised to follow Jonah's powerful God for ever. Jonah sank down and down into the deep ocean.

Floating seaweed tangled itself around his body as he prayed to God to save him from drowning. Suddenly a gigantic fish opened its mouth and swallowed him whole.

Jonah stayed inside this huge fish for three days and nights. He praised God for saving his life and promised to do God's will for ever. Then God made the great fish spit Jonah up on to a beach, where he landed safe and sound.

JOHN'S STORY

I'm John, son of an incense-maker. We live in Emmaus and my father makes the sweet-smelling stuff that the priests burn in the temple twice a day. Some of the plants you need to make incense grow in our garden and it is my job to cut them and bring them in when my father needs them. He mixes the plants with stuff from fishy-smelling shells to make the incense.

Our family have made incense for many generations and one day I will too. I am even named after another boy called John, whose father's job was to burn incense in the temple. He lived many years before me, in Judea, where I live now.

51
Zechariah meets Gabriel

Zechariah the priest was burning incense on the golden altar while the people prayed outside. Suddenly an angel appeared and Zechariah was very scared.

'Don't be frightened!' said the angel. 'Your wife Elizabeth will have a son called John. He will grow up to be a special man who will prepare the way for the coming of the Lord himself.'

'How can that be true?' asked Zechariah. 'Elizabeth and I are both too old to have children.'

'I'm Gabriel, God's messenger,' said the angel. 'I came to bring you this good news, but because you doubt me, you won't be able to speak until the baby is born.' Then he disappeared.

The people outside wondered why Zechariah was taking so long, but when he came out and couldn't speak, they knew he'd seen a vision. All the time that his wife was pregnant, Zechariah had to use sign language because he remained dumb.

Elizabeth and Zechariah were so happy when the baby was born and their family and friends were delighted. When the baby was eight days old it was time for him to go to the temple for the ceremony of circumcision, which is a special occasion for all Jewish baby boys. Here he would be given his name.

'You'll call him Zechariah, of course, after his father', their friends said to Elizabeth.

'No, we want to call him John', said Elizabeth.

'But there's nobody in your family called John!' they said. 'Zechariah, what name do you want?'

Zechariah wrote 'His name is John' on the slate they gave him.

Immediately Zechariah could speak again and praised God for his love and goodness. Everyone in Judea heard about it and wondered what special plans God had for little John.

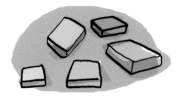

ANNA'S STORY

My name is Anna and I live in Nain. I have five little sisters and I have to look after them today because my mother is having another baby and my father is busy with his work making mosaic floors. My little sisters never stop chattering!

'Let's call the new baby Phoebe!' said the youngest.

'Or Esther,' said my next sister.

'I want Miriam!' said the next one.

'Abigail's a nice name,' said her twin.

'She should be Ruhammah, after Mother!' said the next.

'It might even be a boy!' I said. Then we could call it Amos, after Father.'

Everyone was speechless at the thought of having a boy in the family, so I decided to tell them a story about a very special baby.

52
Gabriel Appears to Mary

God sent his angel Gabriel to Nazareth, where a girl called Mary lived. She was engaged to Joseph, who was descended from King David. 'Greetings to Mary, who has been chosen by God!' said Gabriel.

Mary was frightened at the sight of the angel, who said, 'Don't be afraid. God is pleased with you. You are going to have a baby called Jesus who will rule your people. His kingdom will last for ever.'

'But I'm not even married yet!' said Mary. 'How can I have a baby?'

'The Holy Spirit will make the baby inside you and he will be called the son of God,' said Gabriel. 'Even your cousin Elizabeth is to have a baby in her old age. Nothing is impossible for God!'

'I am God's servant,' said Mary. 'May everything you have said come true.'

The angel disappeared and immediately Mary went to visit her cousin Elizabeth. As soon as they met, the baby inside Elizabeth jumped and kicked. The Holy Spirit filled Elizabeth, so that she knew what Gabriel had said to Mary.

'I'm so happy that the mother of the Lord has come to me!' said Elizabeth. 'When you spoke, the baby inside me jumped for joy! You believed what God told you, so you will really be blessed.'

CALEB'S STORY

I'm Caleb and I'm going to be a carpenter like my father when I grow up. Already I help him by sweeping up the wood shavings and fetching his tools for him. Then I go out to play with the other boys in our town of Magdala. We often talk about what we'll be when we're grown up. Jem says he'll be a fisherman because everyone eats fish. Hiram says he'll be a boat builder because you can't fish without a boat and Sammy says he'll twist the ropes to make the nets. But I'll be a carpenter and make boxes and ploughs and furniture. Jesus, the most important man in the world, was a carpenter. His foster father, Joseph, was a carpenter too and Jesus was born right here in this very town of Bethlehem.

53
The Birth of Jesus

Joseph was a carpenter who lived in Nazareth. Soon his wife Mary was going to have a baby. Then Joseph heard that Augustus, the Roman emperor, had ordered everyone to go to their home towns so he could count them, to work out how much tax money he could collect.

So Joseph and Mary started on the long journey south to Bethlehem.

'I'm tired out, Joseph,' said Mary. 'I hope we can find a place to stay soon.'

But so many people had come to Bethlehem that all the inns were full and they couldn't find a single room to stay in. Eventually they found a stable and decided to rest there for the night because Joseph knew it was nearly time for Mary to have her baby.

There were animals resting in the stable too, but Mary and Joseph were used to that. That night Mary gave birth to a little boy. She wrapped him in strips of cloth to keep him warm and laid him down to sleep on the straw in the animals' manger.

Joseph the carpenter and his wife Mary were overjoyed about the birth of their son, who was also the son of God. They named him Jesus, just as an angel had told them.

TITUS'S STORY

I am Titus, a shepherd boy working in the hills above Hebron. Most of the other shepherds are sleeping, but I'm watching over the flock tonight. Some of the boys hate it. They don't like the dark and are frightened of wolves coming after the sheep. But I like it at nighttime. I've got a big stick strong enough to beat off any wolf and a pile of stones to throw if I hear the slightest noise. But what I like best about the night is the stars. I sit and watch them for hours.

Before we go to sleep the old shepherds always tell stories. My favourite story is about shepherds just like us, who got to meet the King of Heaven.

54
What the Shepherds Saw

Near Bethlehem there were shepherds keeping watch over their flock by night. Suddenly an angel appeared to them and dazzled them with the glory of God. The shepherds were all very frightened, but the angel said, 'Don't be afraid! I've come with a message of great joy for you and everyone else. Tonight a baby has been born in Bethlehem and he is to be your Saviour, Christ the Lord. You will find him wrapped in strips of cloth and lying on a bed of straw in a manger.'

As soon as the angel finished speaking,
the whole sky was filled with angels, singing praises to God.

'Glory to God and peace to all his people on earth!' they sang.

The shepherds couldn't take their eyes off the angels, but as soon as
they'd gone they said, 'Let's go to Bethlehem! God has told us about this
special baby, so now we must go and see him for ourselves!'

They hurried into the town and found Mary and Joseph in the stable,
and the baby lying in the manger, just as the angel had told them. They knelt
and worshipped the baby who was the son of God. Then they went and told
everyone else about what had happened, praising God for everything they
had seen and heard.

CILLA'S STORY

My name is Cilla and my father makes the dyes to colour the yarn the women use to weave into clothes. He made the blue and crimson dyes that my friend Shua's mother used to make her fine new robe. He uses plants and crushed insects to make the dyes, which makes our home a very smelly place! Shua's new robe was so gorgeous that I wondered if it was even more beautiful than the robes of the Magi, the wise men who came when Jesus was born.

55
The Coming of the Wise Men

After Jesus was born, three wise men came to Jerusalem. 'Where is he who is born King of the Jews?' they asked everyone they met. 'We have followed a star from the East and have come to worship him.'

King Herod ruled the Israelites at the time and he was very worried when he heard about this new king. He didn't want anyone coming to take over from him. So Herod got the wise men to visit him secretly.

'Where is this new king,' he asked them, 'and when did this star appear?'

When he heard that Jesus had been born in Bethlehem, he told the wise men to go and worship him.

'Be sure you return and tell me where the baby king is,' he said. 'I want to worship him too!'

But he planned to kill Jesus and thought he could trick the wise men into telling him where Jesus was. So the Magi headed towards Bethlehem, following the star. They were filled with joy when the star shone over the stable and they knew they had found the new king at last.

When they went inside and found Mary holding baby Jesus, they fell to their knees and worshipped him. Then they got out the fine gifts they had brought all the way from the East and gave him presents of gold, frankincense and myrrh.

That night they had a dream that warned them not to go back to King Herod, so they went home a different way.

JUDE'S STORY

My name is Jude and I'm travelling with my father to sell the pomegranates he grows on our smallholding. Every week we ride into town on our donkeys. Riding the donkey is much better than walking because I can see so much more. I can see geckos sunning themselves on the rocks. It's great up here! My donkey rides are fun, but I remember the story of Mary and Joseph escaping from King Herod's men. That must have been really scary.

56
Escape from Herod

After the wise men had left the stable, Mary settled Jesus in the manger again and they all went to sleep. Joseph dreamed that an angel came to him and said, 'Get up quickly, Joseph! Take Mary and the child and escape to Egypt. You are in great danger here because Herod is looking for Jesus so he can kill him! Stay in Egypt until I tell you that it's safe to come home.'

So Joseph woke Mary and put her and the sleeping baby on to his donkey. He packed the precious gifts that the wise men had given Jesus and some food for the journey and they left Bethlehem straight away.

King Herod was furious when he found out that the wise men had tricked him and gone home without telling him where to find Jesus. So he called his soldiers and ordered them to kill every baby boy in Bethlehem who was less than two years old. The soldiers did what he ordered and slaughtered all the baby boys. Only Jesus escaped because he was safely in Egypt.

Soon after, wicked King Herod died. The angel came back to Joseph in a dream and said, 'It's safe to take your family back to Israel now because the one who was trying to kill Jesus is dead.'

So they all went back to Israel. But when they got there they found that Herod's son was now king and they were frightened of him too. So Joseph loaded up his donkey again and took his family to the province of Galilee, where they settled in the town of Nazareth.

STEPHEN'S STORY

I am Stephen and I sell doves near the temple in Jerusalem. Not long ago a girl asked to buy my two very best birds because her brother was being dedicated at the temple. This is our custom of families taking new babies to the temple to say thank you to God for them, by making a sacrifice of birds or a lamb. My mother told me this story of Mary and Joseph bringing Jesus to be dedicated.

57
Dedication of Jesus

When Jesus was old enough, Mary and Joseph brought him to Jerusalem to be dedicated to God in the temple. They offered two young birds as a sacrifice for the gift of a fine son. There was a very holy man in Jerusalem, called Simeon. He was very old, but God had promised him that he would not die before he saw Jesus, the promised saviour.

The Holy Spirit told Simeon to go to the temple on the day of Jesus's dedication. When Simeon saw Jesus, he knew he was the saviour. He was very excited and asked to hold the baby.

'Now I can die in peace and happiness because God has kept his promise to me,' said Simeon. 'For this is the baby he sent to save the world!'

Mary and Joseph were astonished as they listened to him. Then Simeon said to Mary, 'Your son will bring great joy to you and to many others, but he will give you great sadness too and make many people in this land very angry.'

Then an old lady called Anna came up to them. She was a holy woman and spent all her time in the temple, praying to God. She was thrilled to see baby Jesus and gave great thanks to God. She already knew that Jesus had come to save the people of Israel when he grew up.

When the dedication was finished, Mary and Joseph took Jesus back to their home in Nazareth, where he grew to be strong. Even as a little boy, Jesus was so wise he could understand God's teachings better than some grown-ups.

MICHAEL'S STORY

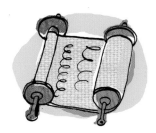

I'm Michael, a rabbi's son. It's hard being a teacher's son! Everyone expects me to be very clever and I'm not. We speak Aramaic at home, like everyone else, but at school I have to learn Hebrew, so I can read our holy book, the Torah. But I'm not very good at it at all! My sisters are lucky because girls don't go to school. They stay at home and learn to weave and cook and keep house. My father says I have to learn lots of the Torah by heart before I am even as old as Jesus was, when his parents lost him in Jerusalem.

58
Jesus in His Father's House

Every year Joseph and Mary took Jesus up to Jerusalem to celebrate the feast of Passover. The year Jesus was twelve was one Mary would always remember. When the feast was over, they set off back to Nazareth. They travelled with all their friends and relations, so there were hundreds of donkeys and carts and many people walking alongside. It was a noisy, bustling group, as everyone talked about what they had seen in the city and the wonders of the huge temple.

Joseph travelled with the men and thought that Jesus was with his mother. Mary was with the women and young children and thought that now Jesus was twelve, he must be travelling with the men. So neither of them missed Jesus for a whole day.

When they discovered he was missing they were very worried.

'Have you seen Jesus?' they asked everyone.

'We haven't seen Jesus since we left Jerusalem!' they all replied.

Frantic with worry, they headed back to the city. For three long, frightening days they searched for Jesus. Then they went to the temple to pray and there they found him. Jesus was sitting with all the teachers of the Law, listening to them and asking the most difficult questions. Everyone who heard him was amazed at the young boy's understanding and his answers.

But his mother wasn't impressed.

'Where do you think you've been?' she demanded. 'We've been looking for you everywhere! We were beside ourselves with worry!'

'Why did you search for me?' Jesus asked. 'Didn't you realise that I would be in my Father's house?'

At the time they didn't understand what Jesus meant, they were just relieved to have found him. They went back home to Nazareth and Jesus became even cleverer as he grew older. Jesus was always obedient to his parents after that and everyone who knew him loved him.

NATHAN'S STORY

My name is Nathan and I sell sandals. My father makes the best sandals in the whole city! I help my mother sell them in the market at Jotapata. There are lots of people selling things – fruits, cloth, cheese, jewellery – so it's important to attract people to our stall. We don't want them wasting their money on pomegranates when they could be buying a pair of Father's sandals! He even made sandals for Jesus, the famous preacher. I heard the story of when Jesus was baptised.

59
John Baptises Jesus

John the Baptist, son of Elizabeth and Zechariah, lived in the wilderness. He wore a tunic made of camel's hair and ate locusts and wild honey. Crowds of people came out into the desert to hear him preach.

'If you tell God that you are sorry for the bad things you have done, he will forgive you!' he told them. To prepare them for the coming of Jesus, John baptised people in the river Jordan. It was a way of showing that they had turned away from their old lives and wanted to start over again. Some of the religious leaders pretended to be good, but John knew that they would never really change their ways.

'Stop pretending to be good, you snakes!' he ordered them. 'Soon someone else will be coming to teach you,' he told the crowds. 'He's much more important than me! I'm not even good enough to untie his sandals for him, like a servant. And while I baptise you with water, he will baptise you with the Holy Spirit.'

The man John was talking about was Jesus. One day Jesus joined the crowd and asked John to baptise him. John knew that Jesus was so important that it should have been the other way round. Jesus should have been baptising him.

'It's what God wants for me,' Jesus told his cousin gently.

So John dipped Jesus down into the river to baptise him. As he stood up, the Holy Spirit appeared over his head in the shape of a dove and everyone heard a voice from heaven say, 'This is my own dear son, in whom I am well pleased.'

JEMIMAH'S STORY

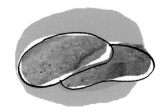

My name is Jemimah and I have to help my mother make lots of bread for the shepherds every day.

'Tending the flocks makes them hungry!' my mother says, stirring water into the flour for another batch of bread. 'It's a pity we couldn't make lots before they came home, but you know how hard and stale this sort of bread gets if you don't eat it at once.'

'It would be so much easier if we could just tell the stones to turn into bread, like the devil told Jesus to do, in the desert!' I sighed, as I flipped over yet another thin circle of bread.

60
Bread from Stones?

After John had baptised Jesus, the Holy Spirit took him out into the desert so that the devil could test him. Jesus ate nothing, so after forty days and forty nights he was very hungry.

The devil tried to tempt him. 'If you're God's son,' he said, 'why don't you use your powers to turn these stones into loaves of bread?'

But Jesus said, 'No! The Scriptures tell us that we need more than bread to live on. We need to obey every word that God has spoken.'

Then the devil took him to the high top of the Temple in Jerusalem and tried to test him again.

'Why don't you jump off here, Jesus, and prove you are the Son of God?' he said. 'The Scriptures promise that God will send his angels to catch you.'

'No!' said Jesus. 'God says we should not play foolish games to test him!'

So the devil took Jesus to a high mountain where he could see the whole world. 'I will give you power over all this if you will worship me as your master instead of God,' he said.

'Get out of here, Satan!' said Jesus. 'The only person I will ever worship is the Lord God!'

The devil knew that Jesus was too strong to be tempted, so he left him alone. Then God sent his angels to look after Jesus and care for him.

JETHRO'S STORY

I am Jethro and my family are all fishermen on the Sea of Galilee.

'Can I go fishing with you this evening?' I asked, as my brother and I helped our uncles wash out their nets. 'I can catch a thousand tilapia in one net!'

'My net will break if there's a thousand tilapia in it,' said my uncle, 'so you'd better learn how to mend it first, just in case!'

'Maybe we'll catch as many as Jesus did, when he went out in Simon Peter's boat,' I said. 'There were so many that the boat nearly sank from the weight!'

61
Fishers of Men

Jesus was teaching the word of God on the shores of Galilee. There were so many people eager to hear him that he was nearly trampled by the crowds. His friend Simon Peter was a fisherman, so Jesus got into his boat and asked him to push it out a little way into the water. Then he was able to speak to the people without being crushed.

When he'd finished speaking Jesus said to Simon Peter, 'Go out into the deep part of the lake and cast your nets!'

'We've been out all night and we didn't catch a thing!' said Simon Peter. 'But if you insist, we'll have another go.'

So they sailed out into the lake. To Simon Peter's amazement, the nets were soon so full of fish that they were starting to rip!

'James! John! Get over here quickly!' he yelled across the water. 'I've got a huge catch!'

His partners immediately came to help and took lots of the fish into their boat. Soon the two boats were so full of fish that they were in danger of sinking. Simon Peter and the others realised that they were seeing a miracle happen in front of their eyes.

'Don't come near me, Lord!' said Simon Peter, falling to his knees. 'I'm a sinful person and don't deserve to be near you!'

'Don't worry!' said Jesus kindly. 'From now on you'll all be coming with me and fishing for men!'

So, after that day, Simon Peter, James and John left their nets and followed Jesus.

BETH'S STORY

I am Beth and I'm very excited because my uncle is getting married today. I've been helping my mother and grandmother cook for ages because the feasting will go on for days. They've already had the betrothal ceremony and exchanged gifts.

Now my uncle has gone to the bride's house to get her and be blessed. Then he'll lead her back through the village to our house. My brothers and sisters and all the guests are all lined up along the path to welcome them. I think it must be just like the wedding Jesus went to in Cana.

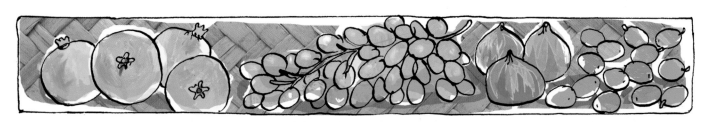

62
Water into Wine

Mary was invited to a marriage feast in Cana. Her son Jesus and his disciples were guests at the wedding too. After much feasting, the wine ran out. Mary told Jesus what had happened.

'There's no wine left,' she said. 'It's all been drunk, but the party is still going on!'

'Why are you telling me?' asked Jesus. 'It's not my problem. Nor is it time for me to do miracles.'

But still his mother called the servants over and said, 'Do whatever my son tells you.'

They went to Jesus and asked him what they should do about the wine. Jesus pointed to six big water jars standing in the corner.

'Fill them up with water,' he said.

The jars were huge, holding about thirty gallons of water each, but the servants filled them up with buckets of fresh water. When this was done they came back for more instructions.

'Pour some out and ask the master of the feast to try it,' said Jesus.

When the man tasted the water he was amazed.

'This is wonderful wine!' he told the bridegroom. 'Usually people serve the best wine first. Guests won't notice if it's not so good later on because they've already drunk so much! But you've saved the very best wine until last!'

This was the very first time that Jesus performed a miracle, by changing the water into wine to please his mother. It also showed his powers to his disciples, who put their trust in him.

DAN'S STORY

My name is Dan and my father is a tassel maker. All the men wear prayer shawls when they go to the synagogue and each shawl has four special tassels. But the poor lepers don't have prayer shawls, just torn rags to cover their thin, misshapen bodies. Leprosy is a really nasty disease and it's catching. That's why they live apart from everyone.

Although the leper colony is outside our town, I often see them in the distance, shouting, 'Unclean, unclean!' to make sure nobody goes near them. They are always dirty and very thin because they have so little to eat. They are not allowed to work, so they have to beg for food. They look so ill and miserable that I feel sorry for them. My mother often gives me bread to take to the lepers. I leave the bread at the bottom of the hill and they come down and get it, just as the lepers must have done in the time of Jesus.

63
The Grateful Leper

While he was on his way to Jerusalem, Jesus saw ten lepers in the distance. They recognised Jesus and had heard of his miracles, so they cried out to him, saying, 'Have pity on us, Jesus!'

He went right up to them and said, 'Go and show yourselves to the priests, so they may know that you are cured of your disease and give you permission to mix with people again.'

While they were on their way to the priests, all ten were cured of their disease. One of these men was a Samaritan, a man from another country. As soon as he realised that his sore body had been made whole, he began to praise God. He ran back to Jesus and threw himself into the dust at his feet.

'Thank you, Jesus!' he cried.

'Didn't I heal ten of you?' asked Jesus. 'Yet only a foreigner was grateful enough to come back and thank God. Get up and go on your way. You are completely healed because you trusted in me.'

RUFUS'S STORY

I am Rufus, the son of a soldier. My father is a centurion, which means he is in charge of a hundred men in the Roman army and everyone respects him here in Capernaum. Yesterday, our servant Cornelius became ill. He couldn't move and everyone said he was going to die. We were all very sad, because we love Cornelius. He's been in our family since before I was born. But today he's just as well as can be! It's all because Jesus healed him with a miracle.

64
The Centurion's Servant

One day a centurion asked the elders of the Jews to help his slave, who was very dear to him, but about to die from a painful disease. They went to Jesus and said to him, 'Please help this Roman centurion, because he deserves it. He has been good to all the Jews and has even built us a new synagogue to worship in!'

Jesus met the centurion and said to him, 'I will happily come to your house and heal your servant.'

But the centurion said, 'No, please don't take the trouble to do that. I am not worthy to have a man such as you at my house. But I know you are so powerful you don't even have to see my servant to help him. I'm a powerful man too, so I know about such things. I tell my soldiers and my servants to come here and go there and they do it right away! All you have to do is say the word, and I believe my servant will be healed!'

Jesus was amazed that the man trusted in him so much. He turned to the crowd and said, 'I have never met a man with as much faith as this centurion, not even in Jerusalem!'

He turned to the Roman soldier and said, 'Go on home now and you will find that your dear servant is cured.'

When the centurion got home he found that his servant was already out of bed and completely well. He had been healed at the exact moment that Jesus had spoken.

JOANNA'S STORY

My name's Joanna and I am a rope maker's daughter. I have a sister called Helah and lots of brothers. We all live in the town of Caesarea. Helah and I help our mother in the house. It's our job to fold up the family's sleeping mats and then to grind the corn for the bread mother will bake later. We usually do most of our chores up on the flat roof because it's much cooler there, but at the moment there's a hole in the roof. I will be glad when Father mends the hole, which has been getting bigger all week.

Sometimes people make holes in the roof on purpose! I know a story about a man who was paralysed. His friends couldn't get him near enough to hear Jesus, so they let him down through the roof!

65
Through the Roof!

Large crowds followed Jesus everywhere. They wanted to hear his stories about God's forgiveness and to see him perform miracles, like healing the sick. One day he was talking to the people in a house in Capernaum. So many had squeezed in to hear him that there was no space left anywhere.

Then four men arrived, carrying their friend on a mat because he couldn't walk. They wanted to ask Jesus to make him better, but they could not get into the house to ask him because of all the other people. So they climbed the outside stairs to the flat roof and cut a big hole in it. Then they lowered their friend down on his mat, into the room where Jesus was speaking.

Jesus saw that the men all had faith in him, so he said to the sick man, 'My friend, your sins are forgiven.'

There were some religious leaders there, listening to Jesus. They were shocked to hear him say this because they knew that only God could forgive sins. Although they said nothing Jesus knew what they were thinking.

'Why do you question what I say?' he asked them. 'Which is easier, to forgive this man's sins or to make him walk again? To prove that I have the right to forgive his sins, I will also heal him.'

He said to the paralysed man, 'Get up, pick up your mat and take it home with you!'

The man immediately got up, folded the mat he had lain on for so long, and walked out. The crowd were astounded at this incredible miracle. 'We've never seen anything like this before!' they said and went away praising God.

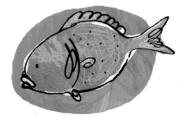

ZEB'S STORY

My name is Zeb and I live in Joppa, where I'm learning to be a fisherman. Ezra is teaching me to cast a net. I twirled round, flung out my arms and let go. Instead of the circular net coming back down on top of me, its hard little weights bouncing painfully all over my body as usual, it spun round in a graceful arc and landed flat on the water. Ezra helped me haul in the rope at the centre of the net, which had caught several fish underneath it.

'Your first catch, Zeb!' said Ezra. 'You must be the smallest fisherman who ever learnt to cast such a big net!'

'Thank you for teaching me, Ezra!' I said. 'I've got nothing to give you in return – except a fish and you've got lots of those!'

'Tell me one of your mother's stories then, lad,' said Ezra.

66
Jesus Calms the Storm

Jesus had spent a busy day teaching the crowds by the lakeside and now he was exhausted. 'Let's go over to the other side of the lake,' he said to his disciples. So they all got into one of the fishing boats and sailed off across the calm lake. Putting a cushion under his head, Jesus was soon fast asleep in the stern of the boat.

Suddenly a strong wind blew across the lake. Great walls of water crashed against the sides of the boat, making it toss about violently. Huge waves flooded over the boat and began to fill it up. But Jesus was very tired and slept on. The disciples were used to bad weather, as most of them were fishermen, but this storm was worse than anything they'd ever seen and they were terrified.

'Wake up, Jesus!' they yelled at him. 'Look at this terrible storm! The boat's sinking and we're all going to drown! Don't you even care?'

But Jesus wasn't afraid. He stood up and quietly spoke to the wind and the waves. 'Be still!' he said. Straight away the wind died down, the waves stopped and all was calm and peaceful once more.

'Why were you scared?' Jesus asked his friends. 'After all that you've seen me do, why didn't you trust me to take care of you?'

The disciples were amazed and said to each other, 'Who can this man be, that even the wind and the raging seas obey him?'

PRISCILLA'S STORY

My name is Priscilla and my father breeds horses. The most amazing thing has just happened to my best friend! I ran home quickly to tell everyone.

'Father, Father! You'll never guess what happened to Elizabeth!' I yelled, before I was even through the front door. 'It was terrible, Father! Elizabeth died this morning!'

'Elizabeth's dead, Priscilla! How sad!' said Father.

'No Father, she's not dead! She was dead and we were all crying and wailing. Then Jairus got Jesus, and he brought her back to life again! I was right outside the door when it happened and afterwards I spread honey on some bread for her and she ate it!'

'Tell me exactly what happened,' said Father.

67
'Get up, Little Girl!'

Jesus was teaching a large crowd of people beside the Sea of Galilee when Jairus, a synagogue leader, came up to him. He fell on his knees and begged Jesus, 'My little girl is dying! Won't you please come and help her?'

So Jesus went with him. On the way there he healed a woman who had been sick for twelve years. While he was talking to her, some messengers arrived from Jairus's house.

'There's no point in bothering Jesus any more', they said sadly. 'Your daughter is already dead!'

But Jesus just said, 'Don't worry, Jairus, believe in me!'

He told everyone to wait where they were and just took his friends Peter, James and John with him. Before they got to the house they could hear the sound of dozens of people weeping and wailing at the tops of their voices.

'What's all the noise about?' asked Jesus. 'Your child is not dead, she's just asleep.'

Everyone laughed at him then because they knew for sure that she had died. So he sent them all out of the house and went in with his friends and the girl's parents. He took her hand and said quietly, 'Get up, little girl!'

Instantly the child opened her eyes and got up. Everyone gasped, then all began to talk at once, amazed by this miracle.

'The child must be hungry', said Jesus. 'Somebody should get her some food.' Then he warned them not to tell anyone what had happened.

ZEKE'S STORY

My name's Zeke and my father is a trader who travels a lot. Sometimes he brings home some strange things. Today he gave me some foreign coins he had collected on his travels. They were nothing like the Jewish coins we were used to.

'Are you sure it's real money, Zeke?' asked my sister Riz. 'It doesn't even have a palm tree on it!'

'It's real enough, just foreign,' I said. 'You'll be able to buy that new bracelet you want and I'll be able to buy a lamb of my own at last! But first we must take it to Tiras, the money-changer, and hope he doesn't cheat us, as usual!'

'Let's go up to the Temple then,' said Riz. 'I want to buy my new bracelet today.'

'The money-changers aren't in the Temple courtyard any more,' I replied. 'Didn't you hear what happened yesterday? Jesus called them all robbers and drove them out! I was up there to buy some birds to sacrifice when Father came home and I saw it all!'

68
Den of Thieves

When Jesus came up to Jerusalem he went to the Temple. In the outer courtyards people were selling and trading cows, sheep and doves. The cheating money-changers were haggling over piles of foreign coins, trying to trade them for as little Jewish money as possible.

Jesus was horrified. This was his Father's house where people came to pray and worship and the merchants had made it like a noisy, smelly market-place.

He took some rope, knotted it into a whip and made them all leave the Temple. He drove out the animals and turned over the tables of the money-changers.

'Get these beasts out of here!' he shouted. 'This is meant to be a house of prayer! What right have you to turn it into a den of thieves?'

His followers had never seen him so angry, but they remembered the verse in Scripture that foretold that he would defend the house of God.

Many of the chief priests of the Temple were greedy and wicked. They took advantage of the people and cheated them. So when they heard what Jesus had done they looked for a way to destroy him. They were worried that the people might rebel and join Jesus and that there would be riots in the city and they would lose their power.

ETHAN'S STORY

My name is Ethan. My father is a barley farmer in Judea and one day I will be one too. I watch my father and listen to everything he tells me.

'You must plant seeds in good rich soil,' he says. 'Make sure they get water and sunshine and don't get choked by weeds. Then they will grow tall and strong.'

Then he told me a story about seeds – one Jesus used to tell.

69
The Sower and the Seeds

A farmer went to sow some seeds on his land. He threw big handfuls of the seed all around him. Some of it fell on the hard path where he was standing. As soon as the farmer walked away, hungry birds swooped down and ate it all up.

Some seed fell on rocky patches of ground, where there was just a thin layer of soil. The seeds grew up quickly at first. The roots reached down into the soil for moisture but because of the rock underneath they could not grow far. They could not soak up enough water and so the hot sun shrivelled them up and they died.

Some seeds landed on ground that was full of thorns and thistles and other weeds. The weeds grew strongly and took all the food and water from the seeds. Some of the little plants were overcome by the weeds and died.

Some seeds fell upon very rich soil and grew to be big strong plants, a hundred times as large as the farmer had planted.

Then Jesus said to his audience, 'If anyone has listening ears, now's the time to use them and try to understand what I mean by this story!'

But his followers were puzzled. 'What does this story mean?' they asked him.

Jesus replied, 'The seeds are like the message I am trying to tell you about the kingdom of God. The seed that fell on the hard path is like the person who hears my message but doesn't understand it. The devil comes and takes away what has been sown in that person's heart, just as the birds took away the seeds.

'The seed that fell on rocky ground is like the person who hears my message gladly and is happy to hear the news. But without roots, nothing can survive. As soon as something bad happens to that person, they forget my message.

'The seed that fell amongst the thorns and weeds is like a person who hears my message but has so many other cares and worries that he does not have time or space to concentrate on it. Everything he has heard is lost.

'The seed that falls on rich soil is like the person who hears my words, understands them completely and keeps on believing in me. That person can then go out and convince a hundred or more people that the word of God is true. This is what the story of the sower and the seeds is all about.'

NAOMI'S STORY

My name is Naomi and my family has a bread stall in the market-place.

'You're good at selling, Naomi; that's the last loaf gone!' said my mother today.

'I heard a wonderful story about Jesus just now,' I said, brushing the last specks of flour from my hands.

'Jesus the teacher?' said Mother. 'His followers have bought loaves of bread for him here before now.'

'Yes, but he doesn't seem to need very many,' I said. 'I heard that when he was on the hillside at Tabgha the other day he fed more than five thousand people with only two small fishes and a few loaves of bread!'

70
Five Loaves and Two Fishes

The disciples had come back from teaching the people and were eager to tell Jesus what they had done. But there were so many people around that there was no chance to talk or rest. Jesus was also very sad because he had just heard that King Herod had killed his cousin John.

'Let's go somewhere far away across the lake,' he said. 'We can be alone there and you can rest from your travels.'

But some people heard where they were heading and spread the word. Many raced ahead on foot, so that by the time Jesus and his disciples got there the hillside was covered with people. When Jesus saw them he was filled with pity.

'They're milling around like sheep without a shepherd,' he said. 'I must teach them.' He taught them all day and then everyone started to feel hungry.

'You'd better send them into the nearest town to buy themselves some food,' said the disciples.

'They don't need to do that,' said Jesus. 'Why don't you feed them?'

'We can't afford to feed all these people!' they said crossly. 'There must be thousands of them!'

'A little boy over there has five small loaves of bread and two fishes,' said Andrew. 'But that won't feed very many.'

'Get everyone to sit down on the grass,' said Jesus, 'and bring the food to me.'

Jesus prayed and broke the five small loaves into pieces. Then he gave them to the disciples to share out between the people. Next he did the same thing with the fishes. As they gave out the food they found that there was more than enough for everyone! Everyone picnicking on the grass had as much as they wanted to eat and when they gathered up the bread and fish that was left over, there were twelve whole baskets full.

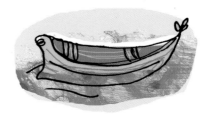

BARNEY'S STORY

I'm Barney and I've just come to live in Tiberias with my Uncle Lud, who is a fisherman. He promised to take me out in his boat on a calm day. But now the day has come I'm very scared because I used to live in the hills and I've never been in a boat before.

'Don't worry, I'll teach you to be a fisherman yet!' said Uncle Lud. 'Just look at that water. It's as still as the floor in our house! It looks as if you could almost walk across it to catch your fish!'

'Jesus could walk on water!' I said.

'That sounds like a good story!' said Uncle Lud.

So I told him the story to take my mind off the rocking boat.

71
Walking on Water

Jesus had been teaching crowds of people all day. He'd even had to feed all five thousand of them because they'd refused to go home and followed him wherever he went. Now it was getting late.

'I'll talk to these people again, then send them on their way', said Jesus, after he had fed them all by a miracle. 'You get into your boat and sail back to the other side of the lake', he told the disciples.

After everyone had gone, Jesus climbed up the mountainside to pray by himself. Night fell and out on the lake the disciples were in trouble. Strong winds had blown up, as they often did on the Sea of Galilee, and huge waves were pounding the sides of the boat and soaking the tired men.

At about four o'clock in the morning the disciples saw a figure walking towards them across the raging waters. 'It's a ghost!' they screamed in terror.

'Don't be afraid!' said Jesus. 'It's me!'

'If it's really you, Lord, tell me to walk out to you on the water!' said Peter.

'All right,' said Jesus. 'Come out here to me.'

So Peter climbed over the side of the boat and started off. At first he looked straight at Jesus and walked on the water towards him with no trouble. But then he began to feel the force of the wind and saw the big waves crashing around him. He was overcome by fear and at that moment he began to sink.

'Save me, Lord!' he screamed.

Instantly Jesus reached out his hand and rescued him.

'Why didn't you trust me, Peter?' he asked. 'Where is your faith?'

They walked back to the boat together and as soon as they climbed aboard, the winds calmed down and the big waves disappeared. The rest of the disciples fell down on their knees and worshipped Jesus.

'You really are the son of God!' they cried.

BARNEY'S STORY

I loved my fishing trip with my uncle! No storms blew up as we fished and I didn't even feel seasick. Uncle Lud taught me how to heave in the long net and then to sort all the different sorts of fish we caught.

'These little ones are lake sardines,' he said, 'but these big tilapia are much the best! Look at this one, Barney. They seem to be attracted to shiny things too. Do you know why people call them St Peter's fish?'

'Yes, my mother told me the story!' I exclaimed. 'It was when Jesus and Peter needed money to pay to the government for their taxes. But they didn't have any because they spent all their time teaching the people.'

72
Fishing for Taxes

When Jesus and the disciples were in Capernaum, a tax collector came to Peter and said, 'Do you and your master intend to pay your taxes? You owe half a shekel each.'

'Don't worry, we'll pay up soon,' said Peter. 'I'll just go and ask my master about it.'

He went to Jesus, but before he could even ask him, Jesus said, 'Who do you think the king should take money from, Peter? From his sons or from foreign visitors?'

'From the foreigners!' said Peter.

'Then the sons will be free,' said Jesus. 'But we should not offend the tax collectors, so we'd better pay up.'

'But we have no money, Lord, and we owe half a shekel each!' said Peter. 'What shall we do?'

'Go down to the shore, Peter, and take with you a line and hook,' said Jesus. 'Cast your line into the water and start fishing. Take the very first fish that you catch and look into its mouth.'

Peter did exactly what Jesus told him. He cast his line into the lake and very quickly caught a big tilapia. He pulled it ashore and opened its mouth. There inside was a one shekel coin, exactly enough to pay the taxes for Jesus and himself.

KEREN'S STORY

My name is Keren and my mother is a washerwoman. I live with my parents and sisters beside the River Jordan. Every day my sisters and I help our mother wash clothes on the riverbank.

'Keren and Martha, you take the ends of the basket and, Adah, you carry the smaller bundle,' said Mother, as she squeezed the water out of a cloth and laid it on top of the big basket.

I quite like washing clothes on the riverbank, although Mother has to do all the wringing out, as you need really strong hands for that. The worst bit about washing is hauling it all back to the house to be hung out to dry. Clothes are so much heavier when they are wet.

'You girls take that lot back and put it to dry, while I wash the rest,' Mother said.

We carried the washing back and started spreading it out on our flat roof, where the hot sun would soon dry it.

'Mother is the best washerwoman in the whole town!' I said as we laid the clean washing out. 'These clothes look nearly as bright as the ones Jesus wore when he was glorified by God!'

73
My Beloved Son

Jesus took Peter, James and John up on to a high mountain. Suddenly Jesus was changed right in front of their eyes. His ordinary, dusty robe was turned into one of dazzling white and his face shone like the brightest sun. To the amazement of the disciples, Moses and Elijah appeared. These famous men had been dead for thousands of years, but now they were there on the mountainside, talking with Jesus!

'This is wonderful!' said Peter. 'Shall I make a shelter for each of you here?'

But just then a bright cloud came down and covered all of them. From inside the cloud came the voice of God, saying, 'This is my beloved son. Listen to everything he says because I am very pleased with him!'

The disciples were so frightened to hear God speaking that they threw themselves face down on the ground and covered their heads with their hands. They lay there, terrified, until they felt Jesus touch each of them gently.

'Don't be afraid,' he said. 'You can get up now.'

When Peter, James and John got up and looked around them, they saw that there was nobody there but Jesus. As they walked back down the mountain, Jesus said to them, 'Don't say anything about what you have seen here today until I have risen from the dead.'

JOSH'S STORY

I am Josh. My father has an inn on the road from Jerusalem to Jericho. It is a long, steep road and there are often robbers lurking in the rocks on each side of the road. I am quite safe here at the inn, but I get to know a lot of the travellers who come here and I worry about them as they set off on their journeys.

It is safer for them to travel in groups, but that is not always possible. But even as I worry, I am comforted by the thought of a story Jesus told, about how a foreigner helped a traveller who was robbed on the road. This is the story that Jesus told.

74
The Kind Samaritan

Once a teacher of the Law asked Jesus, 'What do I have to do to live for ever in heaven?'

'What does the Scripture tell you to do?' asked Jesus.

'It says I should love God with all my heart, soul, mind and strength and it also tells me to love my neighbour as much as I love myself,' said the teacher. 'But who is my neighbour? Is it just the man who lives next door or also people from the same town or the same country? Could foreigners be my neighbours too?'

'Listen to this story,' said Jesus. 'Then tell me who is your neighbour. A Jew was travelling on the long road from Jerusalem to Jericho. He was attacked by thieves, who beat him up, took everything he had, and left him to die in the hot sun.

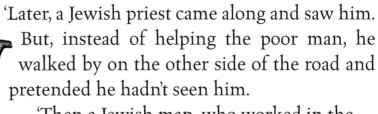

'Later, a Jewish priest came along and saw him. But, instead of helping the poor man, he walked by on the other side of the road and pretended he hadn't seen him.

'Then a Jewish man, who worked in the Temple, came along. He too passed by on the other side of the road, ignoring the man's cries for help.

'Eventually a Samaritan arrived. He was a man of a foreign race, who were all looked down on and hated by the Jews. Although he realised that the man who had been robbed was a Jew, he immediately ran to help him. He tended the man's injuries, then helped him on to his own donkey. He led the donkey to an inn, where he paid the innkeeper to look after the poor man until he was better.'

When Jesus had finished this story, he asked the teacher, 'Which of the men acted like a neighbour to the man who was attacked and robbed?'

'It was the Samaritan who showed kindness to him,' said the teacher.

'Then you must go and do the same,' said Jesus.

SUSANNAH'S STORY

My name is Susannah. The carob trees that my family grow surround our house. My father and brothers tend them and pick the pods when they are ripe. Then my mother and my sisters and I take them to the market to sell.

Although they are only little seedpods, there are lots of things you can do with carobs. People buy the pods to dye clothes and make cosmetics from them. Farmers buy them to feed their pigs and cooks use them to flavour food and make sweets. Although it's fun to nibble the pods and suck out the sweet syrup from them, I would hate to have nothing else to eat! Only the very poorest people use carob pods for food.

But whenever I nibble one I remember the story my grandmother told me of a young man in a faraway country, who was so hungry he longed to eat the pods the pigs were gobbling up. It's one of the stories Jesus told.

75
Welcome Home, Son!

A man had two sons. One day the younger asked his father for his share of the family money so he could leave home. His father gave him lots of money, but the son was foolish. He went far away to a foreign country and spent all the money on wild living.

Famine struck the land and food was so scarce that he had to take a job feeding pigs. He was so hungry that even the pigs were better fed and he longed to eat their food.

'This is awful!' he said to himself. 'Perhaps if I go home and tell my father how sorry I am, he'll give me a job on the farm.'

So he set off for home. Before he even got there, his father saw him coming and rushed out to welcome him back. He hugged and kissed his son, full of love and joy that he had returned safely at last.

'Throw away these rags and bring my son some new clothes and shoes!' he said to the servants. 'Prepare the finest food because we're going to have a party to celebrate!'

When the older brother heard about this he was really jealous and went and complained to his father.

'It's not fair!' he said bitterly. 'I've been working hard for years and you've never thrown a party for me, while all my brother has done is to waste all your money!'

'You are always with me, son and everything I have is yours,' said the father. 'So please be happy for him and celebrate with me because your brother has come back from the dead.'

Jesus always ended his story by saying, 'In the same way, God celebrates and welcomes every sinner who says he is sorry and returns to him.'

DORCAS'S STORY

My name is Dorcas and I live near the town of Capernaum. I'm going to tell you what happened when my brother Sam met Jesus. We were all going to the market-place to buy food and get some water. On the way we loaded the donkey up with firewood we found by the road. Then we went down to the well so that Mother could fill our big jug with water. Sam insisted on leading our strong, stubborn donkey, even though he is really too little.

He couldn't stop the donkey pulling him closer to a crowd of people who were listening to a man talking. A few seconds later Sam fell in a heap at the man's feet. I thought he would shout at Sam for interfering in men's business and I was scared. But, calling to his friends to grab the runaway donkey, he picked Sam up and sat him on his knee.

'My name's Jesus,' he said. 'You must be Sam.'

He was obviously an important man, but his shining eyes were kind and he let Sam sit there while he told a story. Afterwards Jesus gently put Sam down and waved goodbye.

76
Who's the Greatest?

The disciples came to Jesus to ask who would be the greatest person in the kingdom of heaven. Jesus picked up a child and showed him to them.

'Look at this little boy', Jesus said. 'Unless you turn from your sins and become like this child, you will never get into heaven. So anyone who makes himself as unimportant as a little child will be the greatest in heaven. Welcoming and caring for children and unimportant people is just as important as welcoming and caring for me. It would be better for you to tie a rock round your neck and jump into the sea than to make a little child like this do wicked things.

'You must never push away children like him. They're just as important as any grown-up. Remember, there are angels in heaven who look after children.'

159

MESHA'S STORY

My name is Mesha and I live in Kir-moab. My family all work with wool from the sheep that graze nearby. My father and my uncles shear the sheep and my aunts spin the wool. My mother looks after all the children. I have a brother, three sisters and eleven cousins, so she has quite a job!

Often my brother and I hide when she calls us to come inside, so we can keep on playing. Or sometimes one of the younger ones wanders off to look at the sheep. You'd think my mother wouldn't notice when there are sixteen of us to care for. But she always does! I'm sure that even if there were one hundred of us, like the sheep in the story Jesus told, she would always notice and look out for us. Jesus told this story to his disciples to show that he loved his people even more than a shepherd cares for his sheep.

77
The Lost Sheep

Once a shepherd had a hundred sheep. One night he counted them and there were only ninety-nine there. So he left the ninety-nine eating grass and went to look for the lost sheep. He searched and searched for hours. At last he saw a bit of white wool under some bushes. He lifted up the bushes and saw the little lost sheep. He cut away some of the branches so he could get it out, then he carefully carried it back to the other sheep. He sang all the way home because he was so happy to have found the lost sheep.

ESTHER'S STORY

My name is Esther and I live in Bethany. My father grows flax plants then Mother spins the flax into threads and finally weaves it into linen clothes. When someone dies their family come to our house to buy special cloths to wrap round the dead person. It is always a sad time, but Mother is proud that these grave clothes are made of the beautiful white linen she weaves.

When our neighbour Lazarus died Mother said to me, 'Here's some of my very best linen, Esther. Take it to Martha and Mary for me right away and tell them I will come to mourn with them soon.'

I took the cloth to the sisters and they wrapped their poor brother up, weeping all the time that their friend Jesus hadn't been able to get there in time to save him. You won't believe what happened next!

78
Bringing Lazarus Back to Life

Mary and Martha sent a message to Jesus telling him that their brother Lazarus was ill. Jesus was a friend of the family, but he did not come right away because he knew what was going to happen. He knew that what he would do for Lazarus would bring glory to God.

A few days later he said to his disciples, 'We must go to Judea now and see Lazarus.'

'But it's dangerous there!' said his disciples. 'Only a few days ago the Jewish leaders in Judea were trying to kill you!'

'But Lazarus is asleep now', said Jesus. 'I must go and wake him up.'

'He must be getting better then, if he's having a good sleep!' they replied.

'Lazarus is dead and for your sake I'm glad I wasn't there because this will give you another chance to believe in me.'

When they got there they met Martha and discovered that Lazarus had been dead and buried for four days.

'If only you'd been here', wept Martha, 'Lazarus would not have died!'

'He will rise again', said Jesus. 'I am the resurrection and the life. If anyone trusts in me he will rise again and live for ever.'

Martha found her sister Mary and told her Jesus had arrived. Mary too wept and told Jesus, 'Lazarus would not have died if you had been here!'

Jesus was upset at their sorrow and cried with them. Then they took him to the tomb of Lazarus, which was a cave with a big stone in front of it. Jesus told them to remove the stone.

'But he's been dead for four days!' said Martha. 'The smell will be terrible in this heat!'

'Just trust in me', said Jesus.

They rolled the stone away and Jesus prayed to God.

'Thank you, Father, for hearing my prayer and giving these people a chance to see your glory.'

Then he called into the tomb, 'Come out, Lazarus!'

The crowds that had gathered fell silent as the figure of Lazarus, wrapped in white linen grave clothes, came out of the tomb.

'Lazarus is fit and well once more', said Jesus. 'Let's unwrap these grave clothes and release him.'

BART'S STORY

My name's Bart and my father looks after our master's orchard of fruit trees. That's probably why I'm so good at climbing trees. I've got a story to tell. It was the day I climbed right to the top of the tall sycamore tree.

'I don't believe you!' said my friend Thomas, when I told him. 'That tree is the highest in Jericho!'

'Just ask Zacchaeus if you don't believe me! He climbed up the tree too.'

'Zacchaeus the tax collector?' said Thomas. 'My father says he's a liar and a cheat, so who'd believe anything he said! Besides, he's a grown-up, even though he's so small! What would he be doing up a tree?'

'He *climbed* up to see Jesus,' I replied. 'And he's a changed man now because of him! I heard everything they said to each other.'

79
Little Man up a Tree

One day Jesus went to Jericho, the home of Zacchaeus, the rich tax collector. He'd heard all about Jesus and wanted to see him for himself. But the crowds around Jesus were so large, and Zacchaeus was so short, that he couldn't see a thing. He ran along ahead and climbed to the top of a big sycamore tree to get a good view of the famous teacher as he went past.

As the crowd passed by underneath, Jesus stopped and looked up into the branches. Zacchaeus couldn't believe it when he heard his own name.

'Come down, Zacchaeus', said Jesus. 'I'd like to be a guest in your house today!'

Zacchaeus came down quickly and greeted Jesus with great joy.

'I'd be honoured if you came to eat with me', he said, and led the way to his house.

The crowds were not nearly as pleased as Zacchaeus.

'Why is the Lord going to eat with him?' they grumbled. 'Doesn't Jesus know Zacchaeus is an awful sinner, who always cheats us out of all our money!'

But at his house, Zacchaeus was telling Jesus how meeting him had changed him.

'I'm going to give half of all my riches to the poor!' said Zacchaeus. 'And if I've cheated anybody I will give them back four times what I took from them!'

Jesus was very pleased to hear this.

'You are just the sort of person I have come to help, Zacchaeus!' he said. 'Today you have been saved.'

ABI'S STORY

My name is Abi and I help my father, who's a doctor here in Jericho. I look after the garden where we grow the plants and herbs he uses to make medicines. I've learnt that rue is good for cleaning wounds and the tall hyssop is used for treating the plague.

But there are some conditions that even my father can do nothing about. There are many blind people in our town and there is no hope of my father curing them. My friend Zibiah's father is a blind beggar called Bartimaeus. She leads him about so he can beg for money to buy them a little food. We both thought he would always be blind and always need to beg for food.

But he met Jesus on the road one day and now he has been cured, and even has a job! This is the story Zibiah told me.

80
I Can See Again!

Jesus had been teaching in Jericho. As he and his disciples left the city, a huge crowd followed them.

'Who's that going by?' asked a blind beggar called Bartimaeus, who was sitting by the side of the road. 'He must be important for people to be calling out to him so loudly!'

'It's Jesus of Nazareth,' they told him. 'The prophet who is healing people and teaching about the love of God.'

Bartimaeus had heard about Jesus and his miracles and believed that he was the Son of God.

'Have mercy on me, Jesus!' he called out, hoping Jesus would hear him amidst the noisy crowd.

'Be quiet, Bartimaeus!' some of the people yelled at him. 'The Lord has more important things to do than to listen to a dirty old blind beggar!'

But Bartimaeus shouted even louder, 'Have mercy on me, Jesus!'

When Jesus heard him he stopped in the road and said, 'Tell that man to come here to me.'

So they called out to the blind man, 'Come on, you're a lucky guy. He's calling for you!'

Bartimaeus ripped off his dirty old coat and flung it aside. He stumbled down the road towards Jesus.

'What do you want me to do?' asked Jesus kindly, when Bartimaeus reached him.

'I believe you can give me back my sight!' said Bartimaeus. 'I want to see again!'

'You believed in me, so I will do it,' said Jesus. 'Your faith has healed you.'

'I can see again!' exclaimed the blind man immediately, and followed Jesus down the road.

SIMEON'S STORY

My name is Simeon and my father sells donkeys. But I have my own donkey too. One day something very exciting happened, which made me late meeting my mother.

'Where have you been, Simeon?' said my mother.

'Some men came and borrowed our colt, Mother, and I had to go with them to make sure he was all right!' I said.

'Who borrowed him and why?' she asked.

'He was tied up outside as usual, and two men tried to take him for their master to ride on!' I said. 'I told them he'd never been ridden and ran for Father, but he said they could borrow him! Then the king rode him into Jerusalem . . .'

'What king?' asked Mother. 'Why don't you start again at the beginning, Simeon!'

81
The Proud Donkey

Jesus was on his way to Jerusalem. He told two of his disciples to go on ahead and borrow a young colt.

'As you go into the village you'll see a young donkey tied up outside a house,' said Jesus. 'Untie it and bring it to me. If anyone objects, tell them that the Master needs it.'

The disciples soon found the donkey. They repeated what Jesus had said and were allowed to borrow the donkey. They led it up to Jesus at the Mount of Olives

and folded their cloaks carefully on its back to make a soft saddle. Jesus mounted the donkey, which carried him easily.

Followed by the disciples, they headed up the track towards the big city of Jerusalem. Alongside the path the people gathered, chattering excitedly.

'That's Jesus who raised Lazarus from the dead!'

'Lazarus? You mean Mary and Martha's brother Lazarus from Bethany, just down the road?' said one man.

'That's right. Lazarus was dead and buried for four days and Jesus brought him back to life!'

The man looked amazed and stared at the Lord riding by so quietly. Then he started to cheer. The Lord stopped at the top of the hill and looked at Jerusalem below. Laughing, cheering people lined the road all the way to the city. The donkey stepped carefully down the steep slope. Proudly he carried the Lord into his city like a king. Children ran to the palm trees growing beside the road and started pulling off the low branches. They waved them like flags as Jesus passed by. Then everybody threw loads of palm leaves on the dusty path in front of the donkey, as they do if a king rides by. Some people even laid their cloaks at his feet. The people all clapped as they passed by, shouting and cheering.

'God bless the King!'

'Hosanna!'

'Blessed is he who comes in the name of the Lord!'

Everyone was delighted to see Jesus ride past, until they got to Jerusalem. There were still hundreds of people fluttering palms and cheering, but there were other groups looking very angry at the way Jesus was being greeted.

'Just look at the long faces of those Pharisees!' said one of the Lord's followers. 'They hate to see how popular Jesus is with the people.'

The Pharisees were a group of people who kept the rules of the Jewish law very strictly. Jesus knew that many of these laws were no longer important. He would do things that broke the law, like healing people on the Sabbath, and this made the Pharisees angry. Some of them came forward and said to the Lord, 'Tell your followers not to shout like this!'

'If the people kept quiet, the very stones my donkey is treading on would burst out cheering!' said Jesus and continued on his kingly ride into Jerusalem.

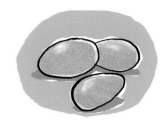

MARTHA'S STORY

My name is Martha and I work with my mother, who's a cook. Today we walked miles so she could cook a special Passover meal for Jesus. My feet ache and all the dirt from the roads has covered my toes. When Jesus's friends get here, a servant will wash their feet, so they'll feel comfortable before their meal. I'm so glad that's not my job!

'The food's ready, Martha!' says my mother. 'Help me carry it to the table.'

I carry in the hard boiled eggs carefully. What I see nearly makes me drop them!

82
Dirty Feet

J esus and his followers arrived at the house to share the Passover meal. Jesus took off his coat, poured water into a bowl and tied a towel round his waist. He knelt on the floor and started to wash John's feet.

'You're next, Peter!' he said to the big fisherman.

'I'll never let you wash my feet, Lord!' Peter protested.

'But if I don't wash your feet, that means you won't really belong to me,' said Jesus.

'If that's how it is, Lord, then don't just wash my feet!' said Peter. 'Wash my head and my hands as well!'

'Now, Peter, I know you had a bath before you came out, so your body must be clean,' said Jesus as he washed Peter's dusty feet. 'All but one of you are clean. It's just your feet that are dirty from the walk here.'

Peter didn't understand why Jesus was acting like a servant. 'Why are you doing this, Lord?' he asked.

'You have called me Lord and Master and that is only right because that is what I am,' said Jesus. 'Since your Lord and Master can wash your feet, so you must wash each other's feet and the servants' feet too. You mustn't think yourselves better than the servants any more because I have made all men equal. You must do what I have done in all things, not just washing feet. You must act humbly and be kind to everyone. This way you will be blessed.'

DAVID'S STORY

My name is David. I'm the son of a water seller. Poor people like us have to fetch our own water from the well. My mother does this every day, carrying the water home in a big pot balanced on her head. But rich people can pay to have their water carried to them and this is my father's job.

Once, two men called Peter and John followed him to a house where the master had ordered some fresh water.

'Jesus told us you would lead us to a house with a big upstairs room where we can prepare to celebrate the Passover feast with him,' they said to my father.

How on earth did Jesus know that he would be carrying water there at just that moment? Father was curious about Jesus and asked one of the servants what happened at the feast. This is what he told him.

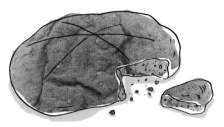

83
The Last Supper

In the evening Jesus and his twelve disciples came to eat the Passover feast together in the room upstairs. While they were eating, Jesus said sadly, 'One of you sitting here eating with me will betray me and give me up to be killed.'

Everyone was filled with sorrow and they asked him, 'Is it me, Lord?'

Jesus gave Judas a piece of bread and said, 'God has decided what will happen to me, but this is the man who will betray me.'

But nobody understood what he meant. Then Jesus took some more bread. He gave thanks to God, broke it into little pieces and gave it to his friends, saying, 'Eat this, for it is my body.'

Then he took a cup of wine. He gave thanks and gave them each a drink. 'Drink this, for it is my blood which must be shed so that many can be forgiven. I will not drink wine again until I drink a far better kind in the kingdom of God. Do these things to remember me when I am gone.'

Then they sang a hymn together and went up to the Mount of Olives to pray.

JONATHAN'S STORY

My name's Jonathan and I help Malchus, a servant of Caiaphas, who is the chief priest in Jerusalem. Tonight Malchus told me to go with the soldiers to carry extra torches. He said that Jesus claims to be the Messiah, God's son, the one we've all been waiting for, for thousands of years! That's why they're arresting him. He's just a man. How can he be God's son? I listened to the men talking as we walked.

'How will we know which one is Jesus?' asked Malchus.

'I'm Judas,' said one of the men. 'I've been his disciple for ages and he trusts me. He's in the garden at Gethsemane tonight, praying with the rest of his disciples. When we get there, I'll go and kiss him. That's the signal. Then you get him!'

It didn't seem right to me, a man wanting to betray his own friend like that. But I'd heard they were giving Judas lots of money for it. No wonder he looked so pleased with himself.

I thought Jesus would have a whole army with him but there was no army. Just one sad-looking man, kneeling in prayer, and a small group stretched out beneath the olive trees, fast asleep.

84
Malchus and his Miracle Ear

Every man was well armed with swords and clubs when they went to arrest Jesus, who was praying in the garden at Gethsemane. His sleeping disciples leapt up, rubbing their eyes, when they heard the soldiers.

'Who are you looking for?' Jesus asked.

Judas went up to him and kissed him on the cheek in greeting, the way men do when they meet their friends.

'Hello, teacher,' he said.

'Judas,' said Jesus sadly. 'How can you betray the Messiah with a kiss?'

Suddenly the soldiers pounced on Jesus and arrested him.

Immediately, one of his disciples came rushing at Malchus with a sword. Malchus yelled and blood poured down his neck. He gazed with horror at his ear, lying on the ground at his feet in an ever-growing pool of blood.

'Put your sword away!' ordered Jesus. 'Violence isn't the answer! I could just ask my Father to send down angels to protect me, if I wanted to. But I must do what is planned for me so that everyone will know I am the Son of God.'

Then he reached down and picked up the ear from the ground. Very gently Jesus put it back in place.

'The pain's gone!' said Malchus in amazement.

There was blood on his clothes and on the ground. But there was none on his head. His ear looked as if it had never been cut off at all. Jesus had healed him. The soldiers grabbed Jesus and took him away.

TIMOTHY'S STORY

I am Timothy and my father is a trader. Today he gave me a great present – a cockerel. He'll wake me up by crowing at daylight. I'm going to call my cockerel Peter because he reminds me of a story my father told me. It's about what happened just after Jesus shared his last supper with the disciples, when he told them that they were all going to desert him.

85

I Don't Know Him!

Jesus was arrested in the Garden of Gethsemane and taken away by the soldiers. Peter followed behind them into the courtyard of the high priest and warmed himself at the fire there, while the chief priests and elders questioned Jesus.

One of the high priest's maids came into the courtyard and saw Peter sitting there. 'Weren't you with that man Jesus, from Galilee?' she said.

'I don't know what you're talking about!' said Peter, and quickly went out to the gateway.

Just then, a cockerel crowed.

When the maid caught sight of Peter again, she pointed him out to the people around, 'Look at that man!

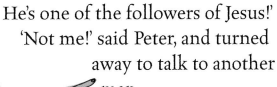

He's one of the followers of Jesus!'
'Not me!' said Peter, and turned away to talk to another man.

A little while later someone said, 'I'm sure you're one of Jesus's men. Your accent shows you are a man of Galilee, just like him!'

'I don't know Jesus!' said Peter firmly.

Then the cockerel crowed for the second time and Peter remembered that Jesus had said, 'Before the cock crows for the second time tomorrow, three times you will pretend you never knew me!'

Peter realised what he had done and went away crying bitter tears of shame and grief.

TABITHA'S STORY

I'm Tabitha and my father is a saddle maker. This is a story I told my brother and sister when they were playing kings and queens. They were fighting over the crown of buttercups I had made them.

'It's a beautiful crown,' I said, 'not like the thorny crown the soldiers made Jesus wear when they dressed him as a king to make fun of him. Give Deborah back her crown, Jem and I will make another one for you. While I do that I will tell you the story of how Jesus died. He knew he had to die, so it's a sad story, but it has a wonderful ending!'

86
The Crucifixion

After Jesus was arrested, they brought him to Pontius Pilate, the Roman governor. He didn't think Jesus had committed any crime, but the people wanted Jesus to die. Pontius Pilate was worried that if the crowds rioted, he might lose his job, so he let the soldiers take Jesus to be crucified.

The soldiers made fun of Jesus. They dressed him in a purple cloak and made a crown out of thorny twigs with sharp spikes.

'We're worshipping the king of the Jews,' they mocked and then they beat him harshly. They tried to make him carry his heavy cross to the place where they were going to kill him, but they had hurt him so much that he could not do it. They had to get a passer-by to take it instead. They fixed Jesus to the cross by hammering nails into his hands and feet and then they shared out his clothes amongst themselves.

Even though they had been so cruel to him, Jesus called out to his Father in heaven, 'Father, forgive them, for they don't understand what they're doing.'

Two criminals were also being crucified with him. One of them asked for forgiveness too and Jesus promised that he would go to heaven with him that very day.

Jesus's friend John looked after Mary, who was filled with grief because her son was being killed. At noon the sky got very dark. Three hours later Jesus called out, 'My work is finished now! I give my spirit to you, Father!' and then he died. At that moment an earthquake shook the ground. In the Temple, the curtain tore open, showing that the barrier between the people and God had now been removed.

In the evening a rich man called Joseph of Arimathea asked Pontius Pilate if he could have Jesus's body. He was a good man, who believed in Jesus. He wrapped the body in fine linen cloths and took it to a tomb that had been carved in the rocks on the side of a hill. Then he got his servants to roll a huge stone to cover up the entrance to the tomb.

RUTH'S STORY

I'm Ruth, the spice merchant's daughter, and I can remember what happened after Jesus was crucified. My father was still selling spices to people in his shop, as if nothing extraordinary had happened. I dropped the basket of dates and figs I had been sent to buy and yelled at the top of my voice, 'Jesus is alive!'

'What nonsense, Ruth!' said my father. 'You know they crucified the Lord! You were here yesterday when Salome and her friends came to buy spices and oils to anoint his dead body.'

'I've just met Salome and she told me all about it,' I said. 'They went to the tomb with the spices and they saw the most unbelievable thing!'

87
Jesus is Alive Again!

Very early in the morning the women went to the tomb where the body of Jesus had been laid. Mary Magdalene, James's mother, Mary, and Salome carried spices they had brought to anoint him.

'How are we going to get into the tomb?' they asked each other in worried voices. 'That stone Joseph put there is too heavy for us to move and the gardeners won't be here to help us this early.'

But when they reached the tomb they found that the heavy stone had been rolled away and they could walk right into the cave. But the stone shelf where the dead body of Jesus should have been lying was empty, apart from some folded cloths. Jesus was gone!

Then they saw that there was someone else there.
A man dressed in dazzling white clothes
was sitting nearby. They were terrified
and crouched down in fear.

'Don't be afraid!' he said to them.
'I know you are looking for Jesus of
Nazareth. But why look for him here,
in the place of the dead? He isn't here.
He has risen from the dead, just as he
said he would. Jesus is alive again! He has
gone on ahead of you to Galilee, but don't worry, he'll
meet you there. But first go back and tell Peter and the rest of
the disciples that Jesus is risen!'

The women were amazed and shocked, but full of joy. They ran back to
tell their friends, who could hardly believe what had happened. Peter and
John raced ahead to see if it was true. John ran faster and got there first, but
he was afraid to go in and look.

But Peter ran straight in and saw the empty shelf where the folded grave
clothes lay. John finally followed him and they both stared with surprise. It
was true. Jesus was gone. He really was alive again!

BENJAMIN'S STORY

My name's Benjamin and I'm going to be a gardener when I grow up, just like my father and my grandfather and his father before him. My grandfather worked for Joseph of Arimathea and tended his gardens, including the one that held the tomb where they put the body of Jesus. Grandfather was one of the four men who rolled the huge stone in front of the cave. But he was still at home next morning when the women came and found the tomb empty.

He always says he wishes he'd been there to see it and didn't just hear the story afterwards. I wish I'd been there too!

88
The First Appearance

The women had been amazed when they went to Jesus's tomb and found it empty. After she'd told Peter and the disciples what had happened, Mary Magdalene went back to the empty tomb, feeling very confused. She took another look inside and started to cry again. Two angels were inside the tomb and they spoke to her kindly.

'Why are you crying?' they asked.

'They have taken the Master's body away and I don't know where they have put it!' she sobbed.

She turned around and saw another man.

'Why are you crying?' he said. 'Are you looking for someone?'

She thought the man must be a gardener. Perhaps he knew what had happened to Jesus.

'Please, sir,' she said, 'if you've taken his body away, just tell me where it is, so I can go and get it.'

'Mary!' said a voice she recognised very well.

'Master!' she gasped and reached out to hug him.

'You cannot touch me yet because I still have to go home to my Father. But go and tell the others you have seen me,' said Jesus.

Immediately she ran back to find the disciples to tell them the news.

JOSEPH'S STORY

My name is Joseph. My father is a scribe and sometimes he has to walk miles to write a letter for someone. Last week he had to go all the way to Emmaus, carrying a great roll of papyrus on his back.

'Why does he have to go so far?' grumbled my brother Obal. 'Don't they have scribes in Emmaus?'

'Cleopas asked for Father specially,' I said. 'He wanted his account of the story written down as soon as possible, so he doesn't forget anything that happened. But if I'd met a dead man on the road, I'd never forget a single detail!'

'A dead man?' asked Obal. 'What are you talking about?'

'Cleopas and his friend met Jesus on the road, after he was dead and buried!' I replied. 'He was so excited he ran all the way back to Jerusalem to tell people about it! It was seven miles!'

89
On the Rocky Road to Emmaus

Cleopas and his friend left Jerusalem and walked towards their homes in Emmaus. They could talk about nothing but the strange things that had happened earlier in the day, when the women found the empty tomb. They met a man on the road, who joined them as they walked, still talking about the death of Jesus.

'You seem to be deep in conversation,' said the stranger. 'What is worrying you?'

'You must be the only man in Jerusalem who hasn't heard the terrible things that have happened to Jesus!' said Cleopas. 'Even though he was the Messiah who had come to save Israel, they arrested him and crucified him three days ago. Some of our women went to his tomb this morning and ran back to us all with some strange tale that his body had disappeared! Two of the men went to have a look and, sure enough, the body was gone! What do you think of that?'

'If only you had all believed what the Scriptures taught you!' said the man. 'They told you that the Messiah would have to suffer and die before he came to glory.'

Then he explained all the things that the Scriptures had said and what they really meant. By this time they were nearing Emmaus.

'Why don't you come home with me, stranger?' said Cleopas. 'It's a long rocky road from Jerusalem and you must be tired. Come and eat with us and spend the night at my house before continuing on your journey.'

The stranger agreed and went home with them. Before they began to eat their evening meal, the man gave thanks for the food. Then he split open a small loaf and passed it around. God had kept them from recognising the man before, but now it was as if he opened their eyes and they realised that the man was Jesus. But as quickly as they had seen him, Jesus disappeared before their eyes.

'That explains why we felt so excited and cheered up when he was explaining the Scriptures!' said Cleopas. 'We must go back to Jerusalem and tell the others!'

KEZIA'S STORY

I'm Kezia. I'm a dancer and I wander around the country with my family, performing in houses and market-places. I tell stories too. When I was in North Africa I worked with an elephant called Juju. People here are amazed when I tell them that. Today a boy, about my own age, yelled, 'What a load of rubbish! A beast as high as a house, with a nose so long and strong that it can pick you up! I do not believe it!'

'Is your name Thomas, by any chance?' I asked. 'For you're a real doubting Thomas!'

Nobody in the crowd seemed to recognise the story of Doubting Thomas. This is it.

90
I Don't Believe It!

Three days after he had died, Cleopas and his friend had just seen Jesus walking down the road, even though he was supposed to be dead. They ran all the way back to Jerusalem to tell the disciples the news. The disciples were in a locked room, hiding from the Jewish authorities. Cleopas banged on the door and Peter let them in and locked the door again.

'We've seen Jesus! He's alive again . . .' began Cleopas.

Suddenly Jesus himself was in the room with them, although the door had not been unlocked again. They were frightened at first, but then pleased and excited to see him.

'Don't you believe it's me?' Jesus asked them. 'Touch me if you think I'm a ghost! Feel the holes in my hands and feet where they banged in the nails.'

They gave him a piece of fish from their supper and he ate it, which proved to everyone that he was really alive again.

'The Father sent me here to teach you everything I can. Now it is your turn,' said Jesus. 'I am sending you out to teach the rest of the people. If you forgive people's sins they will be forgiven. But wait here in the city until the power of the Holy Spirit comes upon you.'

Then Jesus blessed them and disappeared again.

One of the disciples, called Thomas, was not in the room when this had happened. When he heard the news he just couldn't believe it.

'I won't believe it until I see Jesus for myself!' said Thomas. 'I'd have to stick my

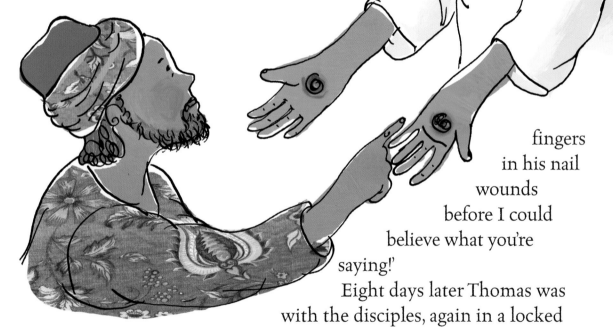

fingers in his nail wounds before I could believe what you're saying!'

Eight days later Thomas was with the disciples, again in a locked room, when Jesus appeared once more.

'Put your fingers into these nail holes in my hands!' Jesus said to Thomas. 'Stop doubting and believe the evidence of your own eyes and hands.'

Thomas knelt down before him. 'My Lord and my God!' he said.

'You believe it now that you see it, Thomas,' said Jesus. 'Blessed are those who believe, even though they have never seen me.'

JAMES'S STORY

I am James and I sell fish. Grandfather is a fisherman and he often says, 'Fishing is not what it used to be.'

'What does he mean, James?' muttered my friend Bo, as we helped Grandfather and my older brothers unload their catch. 'There's masses of fish there!'

'He's talking about the days when he was our age and Jesus made sure the disciples' boats were so full of fish they nearly sank!' I said. 'Grandfather saw it with his own eyes! Once Jesus barbecued fish for them on the beach after a big catch. Grandfather helped in one of the disciples' boats, so he heard it all. I remember it particularly because Grandfather had to explain to me that when Jesus said, "Feed my lambs," he didn't really mean lambs, but Jesus often taught people in stories.'

'What did he mean then?' asked Bo, puzzled by this talk of lambs amidst all the fish.

'I think he meant teach them and look after them,' I said. 'Lambs must be children and sheep grown-ups!'

91
Feed my Sheep

One night some of the disciples went fishing with Peter. They fished until dawn, but they caught nothing. A man on the beach called out to them, 'Have you caught anything yet?'

'Nothing at all!' Peter called back.

'Throw out your nets on the other side of the boat and you'll have a fine catch!' said the man.

They cast their nets on the right-hand side of the boat and immediately the nets were so full of fish that it was impossible to heave them on to the boat.

'That was Jesus!' exclaimed John.

Peter jumped over the side and waded towards Jesus and the others followed in the boat, pulling their bulging nets behind them. There were one hundred and fifty-three fish in just one net. Jesus had already started a fire and was soon busy cooking for them.

'Put some more fish on the fire and come and join me for breakfast,' he said, offering them the fish he had already cooked. This was the third time he had appeared to his disciples after his death.

After breakfast he said to Peter, 'Do you love me, Peter?'

'Of course I do!' said Peter.

'Feed my lambs!' said Jesus. 'Do you really love me?' Jesus asked again.

'You know I do!' said Peter.

'Tend my sheep!' said Jesus.

He repeated his question again and asked Peter to feed his sheep. Then he said, 'When you were young you could do as you pleased. But now people need you and people will make you go where you do not want to go.

Follow me, Peter.'

ANDREW'S STORY

My name's Andrew and my family have been growing olives here for generations. Everyone knows they are the finest olives in Israel and that our olive grove is the place where Jesus chose to leave the earth to return to his Father in heaven. Sometimes I take my friends right to the top of the hill to show them the exact spot.

92
Jesus Goes up to Heaven

In the forty days after he died, Jesus appeared to the disciples many times. He reassured them that he was truly alive once more and taught them about the kingdom of God. But they always had more questions for him.

One day Jesus met them on the Mount of Olives. The disciples were all longing for the Romans, who had conquered and ruled Israel, to be thrown out of their country.

'When will you give our country back to the people?' they asked.

'You don't need to worry about times and dates,' said Jesus. 'Just wait here and soon I will send you the Holy Spirit. He will give you the power to tell the whole world about me. It is important for you to teach them why I died and came back to life.'

When Jesus had said this, a cloud appeared on the mountainside and hid him from their sight. They all looked up into the sky, straining their eyes to see him. Suddenly two angels, dressed all in white, appeared beside them.

'Why are you looking for Jesus up there in the sky?' they asked. 'He has been taken up into heaven and one day he will return to earth in the same way.'

JASON'S STORY

I'm Jason, the son of a yoghurt maker. I saw something fantastic at the Temple today!

'Wherever have you been, Jason?' my mother asked. 'And what's all the shouting in the Temple courtyard? I could hear it from here, but I couldn't leave the stall to find out.'

'Do you know that lame beggar who sits outside the temple?' I said, breathlessly. 'The one with really twisted ankles?'

'I know the one,' said Mother. 'Two men carry him down to the Beautiful Gate every day to beg. Sometimes I take him a bowl of my best yoghurt because he has so little to eat. What about him?'

'A miracle happened to him, Mother, and I saw it! Peter and John were there and Peter healed him in the name of Jesus, their dead master.'

93
Peter Heals the Beggar

Every day a poor lame beggar was carried to the Beautiful Gate to beg money from people going into the Temple. One day Peter and John passed by as they went in to pray at nine o'clock. He called out to them, 'Could you spare a small coin, good sirs?'

Peter said, 'Take a good look at us.'

The beggar did so willingly, hoping for some money.

'I haven't got any money,' said Peter. 'But I *do* have something valuable for you. In the name of Jesus Christ, I tell you to get up and walk!'

The lame man got an incredible feeling in his ankles and feet. Peter held out his hand and the beggar leapt to his feet.

'Look at me!' he yelled. 'Praise God, for he has healed me! I can walk at last!'

He didn't just walk though. He jumped and skipped and ran! Everyone turned to stare at him and shouted in amazement.

'It's the lame man from the gate!'

'He's never walked in his life!'

'Here, come and see the lame man walking! Peter has healed him!'

Soon crowds had gathered to watch the beggar leap and run. Peter said to them, 'Friends, why are you looking so amazed? Be sure that we couldn't do a miracle like this by ourselves. It's by the power of Jesus that this lame man has been healed.'

'Jesus?' asked one man. 'The man we told Pilate to kill?'

'The same holy man,' agreed Peter. 'All you people thought you'd put an end to his life. But God has brought him back to life and it is by his power that your lame friend can walk. Now you should all turn from your bad ways. Trust God and he will bless you.'

SIMON'S STORY

My name is Simon and I'm a gatekeeper's son. Our house is set into the city wall and it's my father's job to open one of the gates of the city of Damascus early in the morning and close and lock it up at night. I was there the day that Saul came to Damascus. We had heard much about him and were terrified. He was very dangerous to people like my family because he wanted to kill every Christian he found. But something happened that day which changed him completely.

I actually saw Saul coming into the city. But he was nothing like the monster I had imagined. He had to be led into Damascus, a blind and frightened man. Of course my father tried to find out what had happened to change Saul so much, and it's quite a story.

94
Heaven's Blinding Light

A young man from Tarsus, called Saul, was one of the worst enemies of the Christians. He was a strict Jew who liked to persecute Christians by getting them put in jail or even killed. Saul was convinced that the old Jewish law was right and Jesus was wrong, so he thought that by persecuting Christians he would please God. Saul got permission from the high priest to go to the city of Damascus to hunt out more Christians. He meant to bring them back to Jerusalem and throw them in prison.

Damascus was about five days from from Jerusalem, so Saul set off on his journey. He was travelling along the road, when suddenly a blinding light flashed down from heaven. He fell to the ground with his hands over his eyes.

Then he heard a voice from heaven call out, 'Saul, why are you persecuting me?'

Saul was very frightened and said, 'Who are you, sir?'

'I am Jesus, the one you are persecuting!' said the voice. 'Now get up, go to the city and I will tell you what to do next.'

The men Saul was travelling with were amazed because they could hear the voice, but they could not see anyone. When Saul got up, he found that he was blind and the men had to lead him to Damascus. He stayed blind for three days, during which time he had nothing to eat or drink.

There was a Christian in Damascus called Ananias. God spoke to him and told him to go to a house on Straight Street where he would find a man called Saul. But Ananias had heard how cruel Saul was and he was frightened.

'Saul has come to Damascus to arrest all the Christians!' he said. 'I'm too scared to go near him!'

'I have chosen Saul to tell people about me,' said God. 'Go to him now.'

So Ananias went to the house. 'Hello, Saul,' he said. 'I've been sent by the Lord Jesus, who appeared to you on the road.'

Immediately something like fish scales fell from Saul's eyes and he could see again. He was filled with the power of the Holy Spirit, was baptised straight away and became a Christian. Then he was known by the Roman name of Paul.

Soon he was telling everyone the good news about Jesus Christ. After a while he had told so many people that the Jews tried to kill him. But Paul heard they were watching the gates of the city so they could capture him if he tried to leave. Some friends let him down in a basket from the high stone wall of the city and he escaped and was able to continue telling people about Jesus.

PHOEBE'S STORY

My name is Phoebe and I'm frightened for my big sister Rhoda and her friends because they are all followers of Jesus. King Herod has already had John's brother James put to death. We were all staying over at Mark's house, praying for Peter, who's been arrested. Suddenly there was a loud knocking on the door. Rhoda went to answer it and then came racing back.

'It's Peter at the door!' she shouted.

'Don't be ridiculous!' everyone said. 'Peter's in prison. You must be imagining it!'

'It's true!' Rhoda said firmly. 'I saw him through the window and I heard his voice!'

'They must have killed him then. You must have seen his ghost!'

'He has a very firm knock for a dead person,' said Mark's mother. 'I can still hear him!'

Rhoda gasped when she realised she hadn't even let Peter in! This is the story Peter told us about what happened before my sister left him standing on the doorstep!

95

Left Standing on the Doorstep

Peter had been arrested and thrown into prison. The night before his trial he was fast asleep, chained to two guards and guarded by sixteen soldiers. Suddenly he felt something shaking him. He opened his eyes, but could see nothing at first because the cell was filled with light. Then he realised there was an angel standing there.

'Get up!' said the angel. 'Put your sandals on, wrap your cloak round yourself and follow me!'

As Peter got up, his chains fell off and crashed to the floor. But it was as if nobody heard a thing! He followed the angel, passing all the guards on the way out. When they got to the heavy iron gate of the prison Peter wondered how the angel would get them through it. But it opened itself quietly in front of them. They walked along the street for a while and then the angel vanished into thin air.

Peter really thought he was dreaming. But then he realised at last that he was free and ran to the house of Mary, Mark's mother. He knew for certain that he was awake when he knocked at the door and Rhoda left him shivering on the doorstep!

Everyone was so happy that their prayers for Peter's freedom had been answered.

'You must all go out tomorrow and tell everyone how the angel freed me!' said Peter. 'Then they will realise the power of Jesus.'

LYDIA'S STORY

My name is Lydia, and I'm the daughter of a dried fruit merchant. My story is about the slave girl who used to sit next to our stall in the market-place. I saw her every day while I helped Father sell fresh figs and dates. I would have liked to be friends, even though she was older than me. But she wasn't allowed to have friends. I didn't even know her name, but I knew she was always scared of her masters.

People would pay her to tell them what was going to happen in the future. But she was never allowed to keep any of the money for herself. One day I went to give her some dates and saw the most incredible thing happen.

96
The Fortune Teller

A slave girl sat in her usual place in the busy market. She saw a crowd of people following two men and went after them. Something made her keep calling out to everyone, 'These men are servants of God and have come to tell you how to have your sins forgiven!'

The two men were Paul and Silas. They travelled around the world, telling people the Good News – that God had sent his son, Jesus, to die for the sins of the world. They told people to say that they were sorry for the bad things they had done. If they were really sorry and believed that Jesus was God's son and had died for them, they would go to heaven. Lots of people gathered around to listen to this strange tale.

'Can it be true that all you have to do is to say you're sorry for your sins and then accept God's gift of everlasting life with him in heaven?' they asked.

The idea made everyone very excited. But the slave girl followed Paul and Silas around, shouting and disturbing their talks with fortune telling. God showed Paul that the poor slave girl had an evil demon inside her that made her do these things, even if she didn't want to. With God's power Paul called out to the demon.

'I command you, in the name of Jesus Christ, to come out of her!'

The demon came out immediately and left the slave girl, never to return. She was so happy to be free of the demon, but her masters were not. Now that the demon was gone, she couldn't tell fortunes any more. That meant she couldn't earn money for her cruel masters.

They blamed Paul and Silas for this. They dragged them to the judges in the market-place and told lies about what they had done. The judges believed the lies and Paul and Silas were beaten and thrown into prison.

RUHAMMAH'S STORY

My name is Ruhammah and my father is a charcoal maker. Charcoal is wood that has been covered up so no air can reach it, then burned very slowly. It is very useful because it burns with a flame that is hot enough for melting metals. When you think about burning, you always imagine flames, don't you? I was surprised when I first saw my father's charcoal pit. There are no flames to be seen at all because the wood is buried under layers of bracken, soil and turf. But underneath it is slowly burning away and making charcoal. My father has to watch over it all the time when it is burning, to make sure no air gets in.

But when the feast of Pentecost comes, even my father stops work to celebrate. He told me the story of how real fiery flames appeared over the heads of Jesus's disciples. It must be a miracle when you get flames with no fire.

97
Tongues of Fire

Seven weeks after Jesus was crucified and ten days after he was taken up into heaven, his disciples met to celebrate Pentecost. This was a Jewish festival, also called the Feast of Weeks, which was always celebrated on the fiftieth day after Passover. Suddenly the whole house was filled with a roaring sound, like a huge wind blowing in a fierce storm. The disciples looked at each other in amazement, because each of them had a tongue of fire resting above his head. It looked like a huge candle flame. They began to praise God with great joy. The Holy Spirit came down upon them and made them able to speak in many different languages.

There were many Jews about, from all over the world, who had come to celebrate Pentecost in Jerusalem. When they heard the roaring in the sky above the house, they all rushed over to see what was happening. They were amazed to hear their own languages being spoken by the disciples, who had never even been to their lands.

'Aren't these men from Galilee?' asked one man. 'I'm from Rome, yet they are praising their God in my language!'

'And I'm an Egyptian!' said another. 'But I can understand them perfectly!'

With the disciples praising God in dozens of languages, it was very noisy indeed. Some people began to wonder if they were drunk.

'How can we be drunk? It's only nine o'clock in the morning!' said Peter. 'God has poured out his Holy Spirit upon us. Now we'll be able to perform miracles like Jesus did! We'll have visions and dreams and be able to tell people what God wants them to do; just as the prophet Joel said we would, in the Scriptures. Jesus was crucified, but now he is alive and God has made him Lord of all!'

When they heard this, the crowd was ashamed and asked what they should do.

'All you have to do is tell God you are sorry for the bad things you've done and be baptised,' said Peter. 'Then God will forgive your sins and give you the gift of the Holy Spirit too!'

On that morning three thousand people became Christians. After that they met frequently and shared everything they had. The disciples performed many miracles and more and more people became believers.

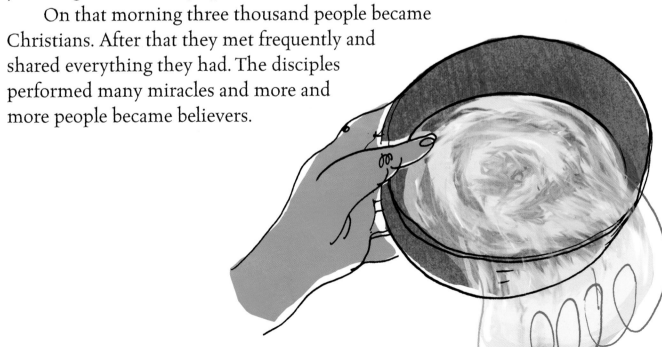

PHILIP'S STORY

I am Philip, the jailor's son. Today everyone has been asking me what happened at the jail last night. I was there, so I know. Paul and Silas had been wrongly arrested, Father knew that, but he still had to do his job.

'The judges say they'll kill me if these two escape!' my father told me. 'So I'm taking no chances. I'll chain their legs to this iron ring, down here in the deepest dungeon. They'll never get out!'

When we went to bed last night, we never dreamt what would happen.

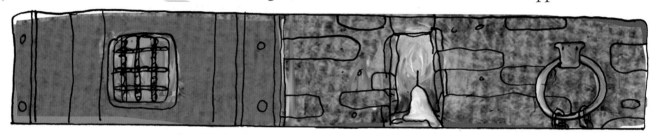

98
Freed by an Earthquake

At midnight Paul and Silas were still praying and singing joyful hymns to God. The other prisoners were amazed that Paul and Silas could be so happy when they were in prison. This Jesus must be a very special person to make them behave like that. They listened eagerly as Paul told them the stories Jesus had told.

At midnight a frightening thing happened! The walls shook, the bars rattled, all the doors opened and the chains of every prisoner fell off! It was an earthquake! When the jailer came running in and saw all the doors open he was horrified.

'They said they'd kill me if those prisoners escaped!' he moaned. 'All the doors are open so they must have gone. I'd be better killing myself now than letting them torture me tomorrow when they find out!'

He drew his sword to kill himself, but dropped it in amazement when Paul called out, 'Don't do it! We're all still here!'

When the jailer saw them, he realised that God must have sent the earthquake to free them. He fell down on his knees.

'Tell me what I must do to be saved!' he begged.

'Trust and believe in the Lord Jesus and you and your whole family will be saved,' said Paul.

When he told them about Jesus they were filled with joy and asked to be baptised. They all celebrated with a big meal, even though it was the middle of the night, and they were still in the prison next morning when the judges sent a message to tell Paul and Silas to leave.

'We've been beaten and thrown into prison without a trial, even though we're Roman citizens,' said Paul. 'If they want us to go they must come and set us free themselves.'

The judges were worried when they heard that they'd locked up such important people. It quickly made them change their minds, as they could lose their own lives for doing such a thing. So they rushed down to the prison and begged Paul and Silas to leave town as soon as possible. But before they left, Paul and Silas visited their friends in town again and told them more stories about Jesus.

ALEX'S STORY

My name is Alex. I live by the sea and we get a lot of storms here in the winter, strong winds – even hurricanes. That's bad for the sailors, but good for my family because our job is to mend sails ripped by the ferocious winds. But some ships are too badly damaged to be mended.

Many ships get wrecked on the rocks near our island. Often a bit of sail gets washed ashore and we carry it home, to be used for patches on larger sails.

Sometimes when a ship is wrecked, everyone is drowned. My father remembers a hurricane that wrecked a ship just off the island, but all two hundred and seventy-six people reached shore safely. Now that has to be a miracle! They say it was because God promised Paul, who was one of the passengers, that he would save them.

99
Shipwreck!

Paul travelled the world, telling people about Jesus. He often faced danger, as the Jewish leaders particularly wanted to kill him. He spent many years in prison, but used this time well, telling prisoners, jailers and soldiers how Jesus died and came to life again. Because Paul was a Roman citizen, he had a right to be judged in Rome, so he travelled there by ship.

It was the season of stormy winds in the Mediterranean and the ship kept being blown off course. Paul warned the ship's captain that it was too risky to continue the journey, but he wouldn't listen. A hurricane blew up near the Greek island of Crete and everyone was sure they would drown.

'Why didn't you listen to me?' said Paul. 'We are sure to be shipwrecked

now, but God has promised me that none of us will die!'

They endured many days of violent storms, then they hit shallow waters. The sailors wanted to try to get ashore in a small boat, but again Paul warned them against it.

'Let's stay and build up our strength by having a meal,' he said. 'God will save us!'

At last they spied land, but the ship hit a sandbank and broke up. There were soldiers on board, who were taking the prisoners back to Rome. They wanted to kill them all to stop them escaping. But Julius, a Roman centurion, stopped them because he wanted to save Paul. Everyone was able to swim to shore or hang on to broken bits of the ship until they were rescued.

The island they landed on was called Malta. There Paul survived the bite of a deadly snake with no ill effects and also healed the governor of the island, who was very ill. He stayed there all through the season of winter storms, preaching the good news of Jesus Christ to everyone he met.

MARY'S STORY

I am Mary and I live in Carmel. My sisters and I often wonder what it will be like in heaven. My father is a great scholar and has studied all the Scriptures. He knows a story told by the great disciple John, who was a good friend of Jesus. It's about a vision of heaven that John saw while he was praying.

100

A New Heaven and a New Earth

'I saw the new heaven and new earth that God will make for us in the future. It had a holy city like Jerusalem, only much more beautiful, like a bride wearing the finest clothes for her new husband. The city has walls made of twelve different layers of precious jewels, gates of pearl and the streets are made of pure transparent gold, like glass.

'The crystal river of life, which flows from the throne of God, runs through the centre of the city. It is there for everyone to drink. On each side of the splendid river are trees of life, bearing a fresh crop of fruit each month.

'There is no need for the sun and the moon any more, because the glory of God is so bright it lights up everywhere. Inside the beautiful city are all the people who have asked God to forgive them and whose names are now written in the book of life.

'When the new heaven and earth come, the past and every sort of evil will be gone and we will live with God for ever. We will never be unhappy again because God will wipe away every tear from our eyes. There will be no more crying or pain or death and peace and love will remain in his new world for ever.'